Passive Income

Proven Ideas Of Side Hustles To Make Money Online

(Get Financial Freedom With Blogging, Ecommerce, Dropshipping And Affiliate Marketing)

Mark Johns

Published By **Bengion Cosalas**

Mark Johns

All Rights Reserved

Passive Income: Proven Ideas Of Side Hustles To Make Money Online (Get Financial Freedom With Blogging, Ecommerce, Dropshipping And Affiliate Marketing)

ISBN 978-1-77485-601-7

All rights reserved. No part of this guidebook shall be reproduced in any form without permission in writing from the publisher except in the case of brief quotations embodied in critical articles or reviews.

Legal & Disclaimer

The information contained in this ebook is not designed to replace or take the place of any form of medicine or professional medical advice. The information in this ebook has been provided for educational & entertainment purposes only.

The information contained in this book has been compiled from sources deemed reliable, and it is accurate to the best of the Author's knowledge; however, the Author cannot guarantee its accuracy and validity and cannot be held liable for any errors or omissions. Changes are periodically made to this book. You must consult your doctor or get professional medical advice before using any of the suggested remedies, techniques, or information in this book.

Upon using the information contained in this book, you agree to hold harmless the Author from and against any damages, costs, and expenses, including any legal fees potentially resulting from the application of any of the information provided by this guide. This disclaimer applies to any damages or injury caused by the use and application, whether directly or indirectly, of any advice or information presented, whether for breach of contract, tort, negligence, personal injury, criminal intent, or under any other cause of action.

You agree to accept all risks of using the information presented inside this book. You need to consult a professional medical practitioner in order to ensure you are both able and healthy enough to participate in this program.

Table of Contents

Chapter 1: What's Passive Income? 1

Chapter 2: How Do You Start? 9

Chapter 3: Youtube Channel 15

Chapter 4: High-Interest Savings Accounts And Checking For High Interest...............20

Chapter 5: Writing A Passive Income Ebook 28

Chapter 6: Forum Posting 47

Chapter 7: Digital Passive Income And The Joys Of Book Publishing 54

Chapter 8: Real Estate.............................67

Chapter 9: Passive Income Idea 71

Chapter 10: Make Extra Money From Freelancing Platforms 86

Chapter 11: Smart Investment Ideas.......93

Chapter 12: Artificial Intelligence..........107

Chapter 13: Other Ways To Increase Your Income...116

Chapter 14: How To Make Passive Income 127

Chapter 15: Habits And The Brain 138

Chapter 16: Selling Stock Photos...........150

Chapter 17: Self-Publishing 154

Chapter 18: Rental Property Investing ..164

Conclusion 178

Chapter 1: What's Passive Income?

Passive income means "earnings derived from rent, limited partnerships or other sources of revenue (in which an earner does not take a active part)," Business Dictionary gives a brief overview of passive income.

The Noodles and Fish team endorsed the topic in Live Your Dreams via Passive Income. They stated that "anything you can invest that pays dividends, is passive income." Anything that you can rent, sell or trade to someone else, be it physical, digital, or intellectual, constitutes passive income. Passive income is any income that pays out dividends, income, and royalties, but it doesn't require your continuous time input.

Passive income allows for you to grow your financial strength without having the need to dedicate much of your time and energy to a secondary source. You need to put in minimal effort to maintain it and keep growing it.

Why do you need passive income?

It is becoming increasingly popular to create passive income. People from all walks are using this opportunity for increased income and to keep their jobs. There is increasing interest in passive income. This may be a reason to create additional income.

These are just a few reasons that this income source is so popular.

It will help you make the best of your time

24 hours is the standard number of hours that everyone has in a day. No matter your gender, age, or status you are restricted to only 24 hours. This limits the activities you can take care of. This is the limit of what you can do each day.

If your current job is taking too much time, you may not have the time to do it all. Passive income allows for you to manage multiple jobs simultaneously. Your regular job is paid, but your money and ideas are earning extra income. This is how to make better use of your free time to increase your income.

It reduces fears of the future

Traumatizing things can result from your inability or unwillingness to pay your obligations. It can lead to anxiety and fear. We are all shocked at the possibility that our current income may not be enough to meet our ever increasing needs.

It is hard to be present in the moment when you are anxious. Fear of the unknown makes it difficult for you to enjoy what you do have. This reality and this thought may consume time and drain your energy. You may also feel depressed if you are surrounded by fear of what the future holds.

The fear of what-if can be a constant nightmare if you find yourself in such a situation. Desperation to fulfill your needs can lead to poor decisions. You are better off having an extra income source than you feel, especially if you're making enough money with your side hustle or regular job to pay your bills comfortably.

It is possible to get rid of anxiety, stress, worry, and other concerns. This relieves your worries and gives you the assurance that your future looks good. You won't even think about losing your job as there is always something you can fall back on.

You can be focused on doing what you like

Many people struggle to make ends meet and work only to pay the bills. While paying your bills on time is essential, it can be rewarding to work for something you love. You can have enough time to follow your passion once you have enough income to cover your financial obligations.

People can now live the lives they want with passive income. Here are the students, working mothers, and others who are using passive income for something they are passionate about.

Many students make their way to school by earning income from their investments. They just focus on their side hustle, which requires less time but pays their bills.

Mothers can therefore focus on their motherhood and avoid the emotional stress caused by financial problems. Students who are able to earn passive income can be more focused on their academics, since they are less likely than students to work after school and to be burdened financially by student loans. It is easier for students with passive income to focus on their education without worrying.

Perhaps you're considering supporting a charity through your time. However, you're worried about the additional time you need to work. Is it possible to learn skills from your neighbor but not have the money to do so? They can still benefit from your support, even if you don't ask for much. Once you have an income source that is enough to meet your financial needs, you will be able to do so without asking. There are many things you can do once you have a source of income that meets your financial needs.

Passive income earners are now exploring new ways to maximize this opportunity. It is a great way of living the life you desire without the stress of meeting all your needs.

Financial Growth Opportunity

A single source of income can limit your financial growth. The only way to maximize your potential for growth is to dedicate your whole time to your job. Most of all, your primary goal should be to pay your bills. This attitude can make you feel cheated. This mindset may mean you don't have the income you need to continue living. However, it may also prevent you from creating a lasting legacy for others.

The other side is that you have the security of knowing your income will provide enough to pay for your expenses. This will open you up to other options. You have the freedom to explore investment options that will gradually increase and grow your net worth. It is easier to be financially educated if you aren't constantly thinking about the stress that comes with traveling. The more information you have, the greater your chances of making a lot of passive income.

Unlimited Vacations Options

It is possible to go on vacation even if you work a regular job. Although you might only be able to work on weekdays with weekends off, are those enough for a vacation.

Even if the annual salary is less than a week, that's not enough money to travel all over the world. Your idea of a vacation will be very different to someone who is earning passive income. The time you have available to go to some places may limit your ability to get there in a couple of days.

While you may feel limited by your regular job, passive income gives you the freedom to take as much or as little vacation as you wish. While you earn, you can have fun anywhere in the world. That's what passive income is all about.

There are many other benefits to passive income, beyond those mentioned in this article. It is possible to reap the numerous benefits of passive income.

What passive income options do you have available to choose from? You'll find out in the next chapter what passive income options are available.

Regular Income Flow

This is undoubtedly one of the main reasons to think about passive income. When you create one, you can make money at any hour of the night.

Passive income is available regardless of whether you are asleep or on vacation. Sometimes, it may be necessary to do minimal work in order for the income to continue coming in.

You can enjoy all these and many other advantages when you build a business to guarantee you steady income. These are the main reason why so many people are putting more effort and time into passive income.

Chapter 2: How Do You Start?

How much money are you going to need to start your business?

Let's start the chapter by briefly addressing money. (I will detail each method later). Online, you can make money with a variety of methods. It costs nothing up to a few PS100. You can be an influencer or digital product seller without much money. Forex is a business that requires capital investment. If you want to see a tangible return on your effort and time, then you will need to have some money.

The amount you'll need depends on several factors such as your niche, what you want to do, how fast you want your career to develop, and of course your budget. Affiliate marketers can also share their affiliate links on forums, social networks, and other places. You can also buy advertising space on search engines for your niche and other sites in your field to accelerate your progress.

Skill-based vs. General Work

There are many different ways that you can organize the jobs on the internet. I like to separate the jobs into those that are more technical, such as coding, and those that are less technical.

These are just some examples of jobs employers advertise. In addition to the general categories, you will also find specific jobs. You don't have to work for other people, especially if it is a job that you enjoy and is well-paid. The important thing is to realize that the internet marketplace allows you to use your skills and create a brand that you own.

You can choose to work completely on content creation, or split your time and work for others. In the next chapter, you will learn how to start your own business. Let's first look at how you can make money online doing unskilled tasks.

Although these jobs can be classified as jobs that do not require special skills, they do require common-sense thinking and a sharp mind. Let's use the online research example. Many people research things online every day, so while it may appear easy or even intimidating to do a job that requires online research, finding the right requirements and doing the research correctly can be time-consuming and difficult. While it is important to be able to communicate with employers, you also learn their requirements and can adjust accordingly.

Data entry is a simple job. However, when you're entering large quantities of data, your typing speed and accuracy will be more critical than when you're typing an essay or email. There are other types that only require you to click or to give your opinion in order for you to make money. Here are some jobs that you could consider general online.

Forum poster

Customer service rep

Website tester

Survey taker

Data entry specialist

Web researcher

Expert

SEO consultant

How to find work/ a career

Begin to narrow down what opportunities you would like to explore. This is important as too broad can lead to confusion. Instead, you'll be grabbing bits and pieces instead of truly understanding the opportunity. It is easier to focus on one skill.

It is important not only to know what type of job you are looking for but also which industry it falls under. In many cases, social networks are a good place for you to start. By joining a forum or Facebook group, you can stay in touch with current news and also find new clients.

Let's take, for example, internet marketing professionals who are experts at search engine optimization. Google changes its algorithm all the time, so a strategy that worked yesterday might not be effective today. There are also trends that can be applied to each industry in order to maximize your chances at getting hired and/or earning a decent income.

The most popular job search engines, Indeed and Monster, are good places to find work. But you don't have to only look for the big names. Also, consider niche job sites and freelancer platforms. Here's the list, with a few niche sites included:

Multiple Industries

TopTal

Freelancer

LinkedIn

FlexJobs

Indeed

Upwork

Guru

PeoplePerHour

Chapter 3: Youtube Channel

YouTube is our lucky era. The platform is still relevant and evolving. And the growth is insane!

Millions, if perhaps billions of videos get uploaded each month. A lot of people prefer videos to reading boring articles. This makes finding your audience easier. Making videos is a creative endeavor, and there is no shortage of people who do it.

It is possible to create anything, including vlogs, gaming videos, tutorials, etc. YouTube lets you create ads, and you can get paid to show ads on videos.

How to make money on YouTube channels

To join YouTube as an affiliate, you will first need to register. YouTubers who upload daily videos can join the YouTube Partner Program, which allows them access to exclusive features.

YouTube does not require you to become a YouTube Partner in order to earn. You can easily create an AdSense profile and begin making money as soon you receive views. The network is easier if you are a collaborator.

YouTube affiliates could earn income from many sources. YouTube affiliates will be able to benefit from a variety of income sources, including advertisements, YouTube premium subscriptions and fan-funded features, such as Super Chat, channel memberships, and YouTube's merchandise list.

Here are five steps to help you earn on this global platform.

Step #1: Create a Channel

It's easy to do and you can find a lot of helpful YouTube guides. Just type in "How to Make a YouTube Channel" to get the next step.

Step 2: Meet the Requirements

Make sure your channel is well-known enough to qualify for the YouTube partner program. To be eligible to join the YouTube Partner Program, you must have at minimum 1000 subscribers. In addition, over the last 12 mois, 4,000 people need to have seen your videos.

Step #3: How to Get Started with AdSense

It's very easy. Simply go on Google and type in "YouTube's official Guide for AdSense Account". Follow the simple steps shared from Google.

Step # 4: Exploring Monetization Features

For instance, the eligibility criteria for each monetization differ.

Ad Revenue - To begin earning ad-revenue, you must have reached the age of 18. You also need to create content that is easy to understand for advertisers. YouTube advertisers will also be more comfortable running their ads on videos that are less controversial. Therefore, you will make more.

YouTube Premium Earnings. You will receive a part of the subscription fees that YouTube premium members pay to view your video. The best part? Everything is automated.

Channel Memberships – To be eligible to offer your channel's membership, you must reach 18 years of age and have over 30,000 subscribers.

YouTube's Merchandise Store - If you are over 18, have at least 10,000 subscribers, you may sell your merch through YouTube's merchandise store.

Payments to Chit Chat - You must be under 18 years of age and a citizen of a country offering the Super Chit Payment feature.

Step #5 - Participating in Current Reviews

You have probably noticed the famous phrase, "With great powers comes great responsibility."

YouTube will hold you account to a higher standard after you become a YouTube associate. YouTube's community guidelines are also required. Furthermore, you'll need to be compliant with copyright laws.

Earn through Sponsored Content

This is more like becoming a influencer, similar to Instagram. This is sometimes called the #sponcon approach. The best part is that YouTube doesn't require anyone to pay any commissions or cut for their sponsored income.

YouTube or any other third party cannot mediate with any brand that pays them.

It is easy to see why it is so popular.

If you can reach a broad audience for a brand, and your videos have relevance to their niche, they'd love to hear from. It's as easy as three steps.

Consider a brand that would like to be partnered with you.

Make a deal.

Be transparent and create.

Chapter 4: High-Interest Savings Accounts and Checking for High Interest

Many people are afraid of leaving their money with banks because of the extra charges they face. Some banks offer savings and checking account interest. They don't charge outrageous fees. This is an opportunity for passive income to grow by earning interest on your savings.

This is true regardless of whether you open checking accounts, which allow you easy access and a savings bank account for depositing money that you can keep safe for a certain period.

A high-yielding account pays 20 times more than the national average interest rate on a standard savings bank account. This makes them more attractive to savers. It also provides an incentive for potential investors.

Here are some things to keep in mind when you search for the best high rate bank.

Interest Rates

It is possible to make passive income with your savings by choosing a high paying bank. Before you give your money to banks, consider how much interest they offer.

There are two types of percentages offered by banks. These are both the Annual Percentage rate (APR), or the APY. The latter should be your focus. It also takes into account the compound annual interest on your investment for a year. This could be monthly. It is possible to get an idea of what your earnings will be within one year of savings banking with them. Your earnings returns will depend on how often you compound your interest.

It is important to note that the average APY on savings accounts is between 0.10-0.20%. High-yield funds offer an APY between 0.10 and 0.20%. Banks offering this level of APY will be available if you do your due diligence.

The interest rate is calculated using $APY = (1+r/n)^n - 1$, where n is the number annually compounded interest and r the annual interest.

The compound rate of interest is calculated on a regular basis. The interest amount will be added onto your account balance. It is an easier way to earn more interest than simple interest.

For instance, if 500 is held in a regular account over a period of one year, it will likely earn $0.50 per cent interest. However, the same amount will earn you $10 if it is left in a high return account that pays 2% annual percentage. Imagine if $10,000 were invested for 15 or twenty years.

It is essential to find out whether the advertised APRY is promotional or standard. Banks may offer attractive APY during promotions or for a particular length of time. It is important to find out the truth regarding the bank's interest rate, before you open an account.

Initial Deposit Requirements

What about the initial deposit requirements. You can find out what the acceptable first deposit is, and check your financial capacity. You will need the minimum amount to open an account.

If you are able meet this requirement you can go ahead with the bank, provided you are happy with the bank's interest rates. You can continue searching until you find a bank that fulfills your requirements.

Online Bank Vs. Traditional Bank

You will need to make this decision. At the first stage, you must decide whether or not you will prefer a bank that is more traditional.

Each option offers benefits that you need to fully consider before making a choice. Online banking allows for convenience. Online banking gives you access to your account, and allows you make transactions from wherever you may be. It doesn't matter whether you need to make transactions in the middle of the night, or at the crack of dawn when traditional banks aren't open.

A traditional bank will offer you the personal experience associated with banklng. Find out if your bank is able to deposit or withdraw from an ATM at another bank. What are the other options if your bank does not support this? Are you okay with them or not This highlights how important it is for you to compare the pros and disadvantages of each bank option before making a choice.

Minimum Balance and Account Fees

Before you open an account with a bank understand the requirements for initial deposits. This is because many banks only charge interest to accounts that meet their basic requirements. The bank might charge you a fee if your balance is lower than the minimum approved amount. If you are aware of the minimum account balance and can maintain it above, this will avoid any fees. Citi Accelerate Savings will add $4.50 monthly to your account if it is less than $500.

Your research should go a step further. Even though the purpose of opening the account was to save your money and earn an interest on it, make sure you check whether there are specific withdrawal rules. These include the maximum and minimum amounts that you can withdraw. The frequency at which withdrawals are allowed and the transfer frequency should be checked. This is a great method to ensure you don't end up in an unpleasant situation with the bank when you need to access your funds quickly.

Barclays charges account owners $5 each time they withdraw or transfer money after they reach the allowed six monthly withdrawal/transfer. If you make these transactions more than once in a year, your account can be closed.

If your bank offers high yielding savings accounts, it will make opening a savings account easy. If your bank doesn't offer high-yielding savings accounts, the process might take longer, but it is well worth the effort.

You won't need to wait more than 15 mins, no matter whether you open a new bank account. Many banks permit users to create these accounts through their banking portal. Once you have filled out the information, you will be able to start.

After considering all of the factors, make your decision and start to reap the enormous benefits of these banks with their attractive rates of interest and attractive incentives.

These banks have the highest Annual Yield (APY) and are worth looking into:

CIT Bank

Vio Bank

CIBC Bank USA

Popular Direct

Citibank

Eric Rosenberg's article, "The Best High Interest Savings Accounts 2019," gave a complete list highlighting the best banks with high interest rates. These banks offer attractive rates and you can choose to invest in them.

Saving money in high yield savings or checking accounts can be a great way of protecting your money and earning passive income. Before you put your money into this investment opportunity, make sure to do as much research as possible. When you find a bank that fits your criteria, rest assured that it is in good hands.

This will allow you to keep earning passive income for many more years.

Take a look through the various investment options available and decide which one you prefer. It is important to research every idea. Don't rush to make investments without thorough information about the potential profit and other relevant information.

Chapter 5: Writing a Passive Income Ebook

Many people have started learning to make money by eBooks. You've probably heard about passive income.

Work now to reap the benefits for weeks and months, sometimes even years.

Although it's not easy, eBook reading is a side business you shouldn't ignore.).

Even though print books still dominate the market, it is easier to get into printing by choosing the Kindle or Nook or iBook route.

Amazon makes it easy than ever to publish a book. A physical book can be a natural extension to your eBook.

This step-bystep guide will help you make money selling eBooks. We'll talk about what to write, where to publish, how to get it published, and other details.

I can only say that it was a storm of the right books at the right price and the right time.

However, eBooks do not make it impossible to be successful.

The best way to increase your odds of making money with ebooks is to have a solid system. These are the elements you must include in your system.

A niche and content development system.

You need to choose the right platform.

How to make the most of your marketing campaigns

Perhaps most important, after you have published your first book, it is crucial that you maintain momentum, not just sit back and relax.

WHAT ARE THE DIFFERENCES IN EBOOKS AND BOOKS

eBooks are electronic books which have been published online. That's it.

It is similar to streaming a Netflix or Amazon movie, but digital. eBooks are electronic versions printed books. These ebooks can be used on your smartphone and other devices with an internet connection.

More eBooks published today than ever before.

It can happen for many reasons.

Self-publishing eBooks offers authors the opportunity to make more. Traditional publishing is labor-intensive and can lead to difficult commissions.

An eBook is simple to create and distribute. Anybody can make an eBook without leaving their home. The market is unlimited.

These points demonstrate that you don't necessarily have to wait until HarperCollins approves you if you are writing a book.

Self-publishing a book can be done on Amazon and Barnes & Noble for no cost.

Yes, it is possible to complete this process without any cost. I do however recommend investing some money in a cover design and possibly an editor. You can choose your price range and market the product through any channel.

Unlike traditional publishing and other forms of publishing, eBooks are able to generate huge commissions. An eBook sales could result in 70% of the selling prices, compared with 1-7% for traditional publishing.

Let's see how to make a living writing eBooks.

HOW TO MAKE SUCCESS BY WRITING An EBOOK

If you are looking to become an eBook author, and then write your next novel, it's important to plan ahead. You need to think about your niche, whether you're writing fiction and nonfiction.

Succession is not achieved by random methods. These are writers or marketers who specialize writing eBooks on a particular topic or niche.

It is precisely why it is so important that you plan your next Kindle eBook.

CREATE YOUR NICHE

Stephen King's niche is something that comes to mind immediately when you think of him.

Stephen King could be your best choice for a horror novel.

If you were searching for historical romance, you would likely do a double-take to see his name next alongside a Fabio Esque gentleman in hoop pants and a swooning maiden dressed in hoop gowns.

The King of Horror, a publishing legend, has carved a niche. You should, too.

It is a traditional publishing lesson that can also be used to write successful eBooks.

WHY IS IT IMPORTANT FOR A NICHE TO BE AVAILABLE?

One of the best reasons to have your own niche is to make it easier to position yourself as an expert in your area. It is likely that you only know a small amount about one topic, while you have a good grasp of many others.

Assume that you work in a general children's hospital as a nursing assistant. It is possible to learn a lot about common childhood illnesses and what it takes for a nurse to become one.

You're likely familiar with head trauma, bone problems in children and heart conditions.

Is it possible to create an eBook about vaccines in children's health? What would distinguish it from the existing literature?

Many doctors and parents are already writing books on the subject. It is possible that you are considered unqualified or insufficiently qualified to work in this area.

However, you might consider writing about how your parents viewed the benefits and risks associated with vaccinations. You could also talk about how your doubts about vaccinations were resolved. You might present yourself to be an expert on both the parental side and the nursing side.

The role of parent or nurse is great because it requires you to use all your abilities. You are the only one who can fill this role, but it also provides two essential needs (parenting info and health info).

After this eBook has been published, you might want to write more books about topics that are not covered by conventional medical advice. Unfortunately, the market has already emerged.

I prefer to go small when it comes down to choosing a niche.

It is possible to write an entire book on how to live a healthier and happier life. There are hundreds upon hundreds of books available that provide information on how to live a healthier life. It is not easy to bring anything new. It is very easy to become overwhelmed.

Instead, you should write for a certain audience. Instead of writing how to keep fit, you can instruct pregnant women on how to remain in a budget. Writing about health for guys is better than writing about depression. Keep your pets safe and active by compiling a comprehensive list.

None of these books are on the New York Times Best Seller List. All of these books can help you make a long-term passive income.

Keep in mind, success in eBooks is at most partially a result of being at the right location at the right time.

Websites as well as eBooks can benefit from this strategy. But, even though it is more common to prefer a less important strategy, it is not always best.

It is the reason.

DO NOT CONTENT YOURSELF IN A BOX.

There is one caveat. Tim Ferriss was the author of the 4-Hour Workweek. This shows that you don't need to find the narrowest niche. Although he is now well-known, he was not able to write on any topic. He started with the four-hour theme.

The 4-Hour Workweek, a popular concept in recent years, is now very much in demand.

The Chef for Four Hrs

4-Hour Workout

These books are full of self-help and strategy tips. Tim has written about working out, cooking, and outsourcing.

Aren't they different topics? Yes, but all of it revolves around self improvement. He expects his readers to look beyond the box in order to find new ideas and will do so in both of his novels.

A niche should not be too narrow. You'd love to see the forest along with the trees.

You can choose your perspective but don't forget to keep it consistent, especially after you've published a few eBooks.

Write more about a subject to increase your authority.

It is critical to make sure you answer all questions. If the reader has to leave your book and go elsewhere, it's not enough.

SEEK OUT THESE QUESTIONS AS YOU EXPLORE YOUR NICHE

Finding your niche can seem overwhelming. To narrow it down, ask yourself some questions.

Here are a couple of ideas to help you think:

What are your interests and hobbies? Even though you may have a lot of knowledge about engineering and law, writing about it could become tedious if there isn't a passion for it. What would be your career if there was a year for every subject you wanted?

What do your experiences and studies tell you about your interests? It's often easier (and more fun) to write about what you think.

What demographic are you looking to target? Are you trying motivation teenagers? Do you want to be a role example for stay-at–home moms? Do you wish to encourage 40-years-olds to go back in school? You may also want to help senior citizens make the most out of modern technology. Is the pet owner your target market.

What would teach you if you could give a day of your time to someone to show them how to do something? Who would your student be? It can help to identify who your target audience is and what niche should you pursue.

WARNING: Take care when packaging the CONTENT

It's the twentyfirst century. It's easier than ever to search for a question with the device in your pockets. Assume that you are going to write about the birds of your home state.

When there are only a few websites offering free ornithological information, why would someone pay money to buy your ebook?

Apart from novels, memoirs, or autobiographies you can almost all of your writings online for free. What are the unique characteristics of the book you are marketing that would encourage customers to buy it.

The packaging can determine how far you are able to write a Kindle eBook series or a single eBook.

How can you tell the details so they are useful to your readers. Your income will rise if you know how to increase the value and appeal of your nonfiction or fiction book.

FOLLOW A PROBLEM - FOR YOUR READERS

Let's pretend you're looking for information regarding how to care your puppy. Google offers information on topics such as "how to pottytrain a dog," "how socialize a dog," and "how I can get my puppy to not chew on my shoes".

You will need knowledge about how to determine if your pet is eating correctly, how you should contact the doctor, and what to do when he refuses to walk on a led.

It's possible to spend hours studying this material on your own. However, it wouldn't be more convenient to simply download an ebook that explains what each step is.

It is this that you should remember if eBooks are to be of benefit to your business.

Make an eBook by taking into account a challenge your reader might face.

That's it! It's possible to find similar material online for free. However, this will require them to invest resources. You can solve their dilemma without taking up precious time.

It's worth noting that consumers will not pay for anything.

It is one giant puzzle that mankind has created, and I don't know the solution. The chances of people reading your eBook are high that they will spend a few bucks. But blogs do not have this advantage.

And even if the same content is online, most people don't find it. Let's not be naive. Niche Pursuits offers a wealth of information on eBooks. Have you completed it all yet?

No! Not. Not if we paid you $5.

Books are almost identical to eBooks.

INVEST YOUR WORK OF ARCHITECTURE

eBook publishing is an example of how money can be earned.

The key to earning money for eBooks is investing in your job.

To make your book professional and attractive, you might consider these resources.

Cover artwork. Try not to draw or freehand on your body. Don't even think about using a hard surface with a Times New Roman label. Hire an artist to design your eBook covers if you're not a filmmaker or artist. You only get one chance for a great first impression. Your eBook cover will likely be the first thing that your future readers see.

A professional will proofread and edit. You won't find any potential errors with your electronic grammar checker, even though they are excellent writers. Although you are usually an excellent editor and can spot mistakes, any other person would probably be able to detect them.

Formatting assistance may be available. Depending upon the platform you're using, there are many options for formatting. If you are tech-savvy enough and not afraid to follow a stepby step guide, you might save money. If you don't understand Microsoft Word, and don't want it to be missed, it's simpler to hire someone to help.

EBOOKS ONLINE SALE - Make Money with Ebooks

An eBook is a digital product at its core, which you can treat as such. An eBook, which is a self-published author has many resources.

Only if you are able to take advantage of the many benefits.

Are you aware about the PLATFORMS

There are many options for publishing your eBook. Here's a list of some of the more well-known.

AMAZON KINDLESELF PUBLISHING

Amazon's Kindle Direct Publishing has been called the "holy grail" of eBook publishing. It is not only the most widely-known, but also it controls more than two-thirds in the eBook-purchasing sector. There are many other benefits.

First, everyone can download the Kindle software on any device. Even if they don't have a Kindle this means that anyone can read your Kindle novel.

KDP offers discounts. KDP also has a giveaway program that gives away books for free.

This isn't a negative eBook money-making strategy. You will create excitement which will pay off handsomely for the future.

Amazon's collaborations with Audible also allow you the possibility of making an audio recording. You know that I enjoy audiobooks and this would be a great fit for your book. It's possible to publish multiple versions of your book, including a digital, printed, and an audio edition, on one website.

NOOK

The Barnes and Noble Nook reader can be called "The Nook". This device accounts to roughly a fifth the e-readership.

One of the best things about writing on the Nook site is the ease with which you can collaborate. Co-writing a novel together gives you something to think about. Nook offers live chat services if you need help.

The royalty rate for books priced between $9.99 and $2.99 is 65 percent. Books priced above this range will receive 40 percent.

eBooks Publishing through eBooks guarantees that job seekers can access the Apple bookshop from any device with an iPhone or iPad. This interface can be more difficult than any other.

It's a good choice regardless of whether your publication is a cookbook, an assortment of children's literature, or an eBook with lots of multimedia. There are no listing expenses and royalties equal 70% of the selling prices.

PLATFORMS ADDITIONAL

Other than the major three, smaller publishers and businesses may be able to offer a profitable match for your book. Smash words distributes eBooks and Nook books, for instance.

Kobo offers a quick way to download books. In collaboration with American Booksellers Association, you can distribute the book to thousands independent e-bookstores.

Scribd is another growing epublishing website. Scribd allows writers and editors to post in many formats. It saves you time, as well as your resources. Do your research. Making money with eBooks requires you to choose the best combination of publishing channels.

SELLING EBOOKS will make you a lot more money.

Writing a book takes little effort. Publishing eBooks is how authors make their living. This is where the hard part comes in.

Here are some strategies to help you ensure that your earnings keep coming in.

Let THE WORD SHOUT ABOUT your WORK

You will need to sell the company to increase revenue. It may begin even if you have only a glimmer of an eBook.

Perhaps you have an online forum that covers your favorite subject.

Don't be alarmed if yours isn't. You can still start marketing after or before you post.

SET UP A BLOG

Affiliate programs help bloggers make money. You may be familiar with this, but it is a great way for people to read and buy your eBook.

It's better to have a blog running before you start writing an ebook. This allows you to gauge interest and build excitement.

Small previews of the eBook are published. The publication date is hyped. Context information is also provided. After the eBook is published, remember to keep it safe.

Concentrate your blog posts around your eBook to increase traction, and maintain enthusiasm for the subjects.

Chapter 6: Forum Posting

If you enjoy talking, posting on forums is one of the most effective ways to make money online.

2A lot of webmasters now hire people to post in their forums to make them more popular and active. They feel that their forums will look more popular and attract more visitors over time.

If you are posting to forums, you only need to create new threads or reply to existing ones and keep the conversation alive. This can be done through interesting thoughts or thought-provoking discussion, as well as teaching people. Another great thing about this job? You get to learn something new. If you post in the forums that you are already interested in, you can get paid to have a lot of fun.

Here are some steps you should take to become a forum poster:

* Browse through freelancing platforms such as Guru.com. Odesk.com. * Search for forums posting jobs on these sites

* If you are called to interview, promptly respond to the buyer. * Reach an agreement on the pay per posting and the deadline

* Finish the job within the timeframe agreed upon

How much profit can I make posting on forums?

You will earn $0.10 to $0.50 for each post on the forum. This can allow you to earn $100 per hour if your job allows you to dedicate enough time each day. You can do what you want every day and then mix it up with suggestions from our lists.

FORUM MODERATOR

Forum moderators will need to be around as long forums exist. This is because forum administrators need people to monitor and block spam, answer questions and provide feedback to forum users. You will be responsible for monitoring comments posted by forum users, deleting spam, answering questions from users and responding to their messages. You would encourage threads and add new content.

This could be an interesting thing to do if there is a particular forum that interests you. As with forum posting, there is also the possibility to learn a lot. Here are some steps you should take to become a forum manager.

You can create a profile for freelancing sites, such as Guru.com, Elance.com, or Odesk.com. Define your interests, and your level of expertise.

* Browse for forum moderator posts on the same sites and submit your application. * Search the Google Forum Moderation Job Openings.

* You can check with the owners of forums you're interested to join. Many people do not post.

Freelancing sites, but prefer to hire people who write a lot.

How much profit can I make from moderating forum?

Based on your work experience and position, you could earn $5-20 an hour. For your resume to be complete, you might want to start low.

Facebook fan pages templates created

Facebook Fan Page advertising is essential for many companies. You have the option to follow the Facebook instructions, or you could download Facebook templates that will make your job much easier. These steps will help you make more money with Facebook Fan Page advertising.

* Make a Facebook Fan Page to support local businesses.

* Email them and show what you've done. Let them understand that they can buy it if they're interested.

* Flip the web site.

How much money do I have?

The site will cost you between $200 to $500. In addition, you might consider charging a monthly maintenance fee.

Submit links on behalf of another to Social Bookmarking Sites:

Webmasters can find it difficult to keep their sites competitive and visible online due to the sheer number of websites available. Website owners might submit their websites on social networking sites to help increase their traffic and attract more people to their site. For a small fee they may hire a professional to submit their sites.

They can also share their website links via various Social Bookmarking platforms.

Here are some steps that you can follow in order to submit links via Social Bookmarking sites to other people's websites.

* Create a directory of quality Social Bookmarking Sites with active members. You can search for "popular" social bookmarking sites.

* Set a fee structure and determine a way to collect payment.

* Try to reach as many customers and clients as possible. Start advertising your book in social networks.

It is important to submit website links on-time. You will provide clients with reports detailing the number of sites that you submitted and which links you have created.

How much can social bookmarking make me?

You can earn as little as $10 for each set of 100 Social Bookmarks. Your expertise will gradually increase the rate you charge.

Article writing

Writing articles for websites is a way to make money as a writer. Many website owners know they must keep their websites updated and current. However, they don't have the time nor the ability to continuously create new content. So they hire others to write for them.

Here are some steps you should take to become a content author:

* Create a profile and post it on freelancing sites Guru.com.

Describe your interests.

* Browse the same sites for freelancing jobs and apply for writing positions. * Google "writer job openings".

* Ask website owners if you are interested in writing for their websites.

What is the maximum I can make writing?

* Content writing jobs range from $1 to $100+ depending upon the length of your article and your level of expertise. Premiums can be offered if you are an expert on the topic that you are writing about.

* Even if writing is not your first job, you can make as much as $.50 for every 100 words of an article.

Chapter 7: Digital Passive Income and the Joys Of Book Publishing

"Write to the right reasons. Kerry Wilkinson

Passive income is an income stream that does not require any effort. Passive income isn't as productive as active income. This is because passive income doesn't require any time or skills to generate income. One can earn money while sleeping or working in an office 9-5 job. It's simple and automatic. You don't even have to work except to create the content.

This is one reason why passive income is so popular. A passive income option is often preferred by women who want more time with their children and family than a 9-5 work job. They want to be financially stable and have time for their children while also earning a steady income stream. It is not easy to earn a steady source of income. This blog will give you realistic methods to generate a steady passive income through something you love. This blog will explain how millionaire women became financially independent and the steps they took.

Self-Publishing

Self-publishing, one of the best ways to generate passive digital income is possible. Because of the advancements in technology, self-publishing has become a household word for people who love writing and reading. Before self-publishing was popular, writers and authors had limited options when it came to publishing books. But self-publishing has made the publishing industry more accessible. Writers don't have go through the tedious steps of being accepted at a traditional publishing house. This has made it easier to self publish their work. What exactly is selfpublishing?

Self-publishing is when media are published by their creators without the aid of established publishing houses or companies. It is often used to mean written media, such as magazines and books. It can also be used as a term for other media, like videos, books, magazines, pamphlets or brochures. If a writer or author wishes to self-publish his/her works, he/she must write the book as well as design it, format it, edit it, and publish it. An author can self-publish a book to receive higher book royalty rates and full creative control over its publication. As a self-published writer, you are responsible for all aspects of the production and writing process. All book rights and costs will be at your expense. However, this does not mean that you must do all the work. It only means that you will have to finance and manage all the tasks.

Let's start by defining self-publishing. It is important for authors to remember that they were not always able to self-publish their books. The publishing process has changed in many ways through self-publication.

The first printing press was developed in 1440. It was an innovative technology that allowed books to be made and distributed. It was the foundation of the modern publishing industry. The traditional publishers acquired certain rights from the writers in order to publish works. This practice continues to be followed today. They act like gatekeepers and decide which books are distributed widely and which are not. This takes away power from the storytellers. However, the digital revolution transformed the publishing industry.

The 1990s saw the official start of self-publishing. The technology to print-on demand and desktop publishing was invented during this time. eBooks also began being sold online. The iPhone was then released by Apple, while Amazon launched the Kindle eReader. These devices have forever changed the way people read and write books. The self-publishing sector is poised for the next wave. This means direct sales from author-to-reader.

Types of self publishing

Self-publishing has become easier than ever thanks to the introduction of small printing runs, digital presses, and the knowledge of publication partners. You can now self-publish a novel, factual book or poetry, regardless of its subject matter.

However, not all books are suitable for self-publishing. Here are some popular self-publishing methods:

Poetry collection - Today only a few large publishing houses will publish collections of poetry from a particular author. There are many ways you can get your poetry collection published. Self-publication may be the best way to publish a collection of poetry. Self-publication can prove to be very beneficial if you are looking for ways to sell copies at public readings or open mics. It is strongly recommended that you are familiar with the current industry etiquette regarding the writings you have published before you self publish it.

Mixed genre collection - Self-publishing can be a great option if you're looking for a book that includes essays, stories, poetry, and so on. This is because these books are more difficult to market than traditional ones.

Stories that need to tell - There is no shortage of stories that deserve to be told. You may want to share information with people about a case in high-profile court that is not well known but which has personal significance for you. Perhaps your grandfather's story is one you would like to share and keep in print. Although big publications might not be interested, self publishing such stories can provide some emotional satisfaction.

Niche market Books - You may have a blog that chronicles a rare illness or you might write about it regularly. Now you want your blog to be a book. Self-publishing provides a way to convey your thoughts. You might find it important, even though your audience is not large. Maybe you are vegan and want others to see your low-carb slow cooker recipe. A book could be published on the subject if it is something you are passionate about, even though it may not have a large market.

Regional market books- A great way of selling books in a region is to tap into its "branding". Are you really interested finding the best restaurants around your city? Or the folklore of a given area. Or perhaps the hiking trails of a specific city. A good way to sell books is to self-publish them in regional market. This is because major publishing houses avoid publishing books that won't sell outside of their region. There are many tourist spots, libraries, book stores, and bookstores that may be willing or able to sell self-published books based in the region.

Projects of other lengths – If you want to sell your 150,000 word novel or your 30,000 word memoir, a publisher might say that there's no market for it. It might not even sell. They may not be willing publish it. You can still attract an audience. If you're motivated and enthusiastic about the idea, you can accomplish it.

How to Self-Publish

Self-publishing is attractive to authors as well as writers. A majority of authors are overwhelmed by the process. This includes how to get a good idea for a book, how best to do it properly, and how much it would cost. This blog will show you how to self-publish your books.

Writing a novel is not an easy task. There will be times when writing a book is difficult. After feeling frustrated, procrastination can be used to help you get nowhere. In addition to this, it can be challenging to create a solid idea for your novel. Before you begin to write your book, it's a good idea that you have a writing plan. Here are some guidelines to help you make a book that will be worthwhile publishing.

A outline can help you get started: An outline will help you to organize your ideas and give you direction.

Set up a writing area. This can act as your blanket.

Establish a routine for writing. Write at a given time every day. Continue to do this, and it will become a daily habit. This will help you create a book that is more authentic.

Get a planner: A calendar will help you organize your goals for the week and the day.

Get some feedback before you publish your book. A lot of feedback is necessary to be able to successfully publish any non-fiction work or anything creative or factual. You should have feedback as well, because even though your draft may be perfect, others might find it confusing. It could be that other people aren't as interested as you were. Also, it is possible to detect grammatical and typing errors with fresh eyes.

Your book title should be chosen after your first draft is complete. Keep your title brief and simple. It should provide a clear picture of the contents that readers will receive. If you're looking for ideas for your book title, the following questions might help:

Does your title invoke an emotional response?

It is possible to see it in a thumbnail.

Is your book capable of solving a complex problem?

How does a title affect someone's lifestyle?

Is it possible for your title to teach someone a skill which is highly in demand?

Edit your manuscript. A professional editor can make the distinction between a fantastic book and a poor one. Make sure you fix any basic errors before you submit your work to an editor. Once you have completed the task, hire a professional. Begin by looking in your own network. If that fails, you might be able to find someone online.

Designing the book cover - This is one of the most important aspects to help you sell books as a self-publisher. Your book cover is the first thing your readers will see. This will make it easy for them to decide whether or not they want to purchase the book. It is crucial to make your book cover stand out from the rest. So what is a good cover for a book?

The design should be appropriate for your target audience. An example: If your book is faith-based it's not sensible to have a cover that is too dark or devilish.

Professional book designers know what kinds of covers work. They know the industry well and which covers are most successful.

Simplicity helps people understand what your book stands for. You should keep the cover design simple. This will draw more people to your book.

Your KDP account - Publishing your work with Amazon's Kindle Direct Publishing is one of the easiest ways to self publish. KDP is an author platform that allows you to create, manage, and publish your Kindle audiobooks. You can upload work to the platform and post it free of charge. With a click, the interested readers can either print it out or buy the eBook. Log in with your Amazon account to create your KDP profile. You can then enter your tax information. Finally, hit "Finished" and your account will be complete.

Self-publish your ebook - Once you feel your book is ready for the public, you may upload it to KDP. After you upload the manuscript file, select seven keywords to make it easy for your target audience to find your book via Amazon search. Once your file is uploaded, you can choose seven keywords to help you find your book when you search Amazon.

Ghostwriting is a method of self-publishing

Today, there are many publishing options and writing tools available. Ghostwriting, one of these options, is available. Ghostwriting is a process where you pay someone to write for a book and you are named the author. It is when someone else writes content for you, but the book is still published under your name. Ghostwriters often have the ability to handle multiple projects of various genres. First, you need to check their experience before you hire a Ghostwriter. Use freelancing websites to find someone to hire. Before you contact them about negotiating a rate, be sure to review their work and look into their past experiences. For as little as $25 per hour, a professional ghostwriter will charge anywhere from $25 to $100. It will vary depending on what services are needed and how many words the book contains.

A ghostwriter can bring you many benefits.

You might get a better quality piece of writing. It is easier to write for professionals ghostwriters because they are more naturally talented writers. Expcct a higher level.

Since someone else will handle it, you don't have to spend much time sitting down at a computer. However, you must spend time giving feedback to the ghostwriter and providing suggestions, adequate notes, reviewing their writing, then waiting for the changes.

You can hire native writers to help with writing a book if the language is not your first. This is especially true when you don't speak English well enough to write the book. To overcome this language barrier and create a book that makes meaning, you may hire a ghostwriter.

Now that your understanding of self-publishing has been established, go ahead to create the book you always wanted and share it all with the world.

Chapter 8: Real Estate

This one is most likely familiar to you. Unless society has made you a hostile environment with its bizarre concrete structures, then you probably live in either a home that you own or rented. Passive income from realty has been around since the beginning because shelter is something that we all need.

It is not easy to afford real estate. It's worth thinking about. You have many options when it comes to investing in real-estate.

* Single-Family Housing (SFH). This is a separate rental property, which can be purchased as a condo or house. It is usually rented out to a single tenant. A SFH is a common choice for real property investment. However, they are also risky since landlords could lose income due turnovers or vacancies.

* Multi-Family Unites (MFU): Usually a quadplex, triplex, duplex or quadplex that has multiple tenants. This unit generates more revenues than an SFH. An alternative to buying

multiple SFHs is to have one mortgage and one property bill.

* Apartment Buildings: A more substantial investment than MFUs, but equally as straightforward. This type of property can bring in more revenue but it will require more complex management. Therefore, hiring a property administrator is the best.

* Storage units/Facilities are characterized by low overheads and high demand from customers who need additional storage space. Higher revenue means more units. You might need insurance, security, or property management.

* Vacation Homes: These properties are perfect for vacationers as they are located in the most beautiful areas of nature. These homes can be rented to your family for low seasons or used by you and your family when the demand rises.

* Commercial properties - require greater investment and startup. Partners with other investors are recommended.

How much money can you spend when you invest in real estate? As you can see, many of these options come with high prices. Your first investment should be modest. For the best possible investment, make sure you only buy properties at 70% of their actual market value. When money starts to flow in, you can upgrade or remodel the property you already own.

Location matters when you are buying a home. The location of a home is an important factor in any aspect of real property, but this one is different. Homes in good neighborhoods or close to schools tends be more valuable than those that aren't. This allows renters to charge higher rents, or sellers to receive a decent return on their investment.

Different areas will also attract different tenants. The home will attract many professionals if it is located near major roads or highways. It will also attract many retired people if it is located in rural areas or suburbs. The first step to determining the location of your property is to identify what kind of property you want and how long you intend to keep it.

If you are going to be flipping houses, it's worth looking at foreclosures to increase your profits. You can often find amazing deals that will allow you to make the most of your investment after renovating and purchasing. You should not rent to fixer-uppers, whether you are renting to professionals, couples, and families. These tenants seek a solution that is complete and ready to move in. The property should be fully furnished and ready for tenants to move in.

Tenants are the lifeblood and soul of any rental company. Your bottom line will be happier if they're happy. You should pay attention to their concerns and requirements, respond quickly and communicate clearly. You need to show them that you are available for assistance if they have any problems. This can sometimes prove costly, so it is worth hiring a property manger to manage your affairs.

Chapter 9: Passive Income Idea

1. Rent Real Estate

This chapter shows you how to start passively making money by renting out real-estate. It's simple, consistent, and very promising. Your first question might be, "Can I earn money by renting real property?" Absolutely! It's possible to passively make good money renting out real estate. It is available to anyone.

Next question is "How?"

Consider the assets you might own that you inherited from your ancestors. This is the best choice for you.

Ways To Rent Real Estate:

Real estate property is one among the most valuable assets you could own. You can rent all the spaces that you own to qualified tenants. This allows you the possibility to rent your property for residential or commercial purposes. If your property has a good or excellent location and is highly sought-after, you can charge a reasonable rent.

Two options are available to you: You may rent space for both residential and commercial purposes. These two options are described below:

Rent a Residential Apartment

A retired vet might be looking for a home near the city and their children's school. However, an empty house or apartment in the area could be their best chance. Renting your apartment to a reliable family is a great way to earn some side income. Your best bet is to start by asking for a fair price and using the full potential of your house's layout and architecture. A family that feels your terms are fair and feasible for their lives will not hesitate to accept your terms.

A nice room in an apartment can be rented out to make money. Many people are unable to afford a home and need their own private space. The only thing you have to do is to find a paying guest (or a suitor) who will pay for the place and share some of their utility bills. An ideal tenant could be a international student looking for a place to call home, a temporary employee of a corporation, or someone who just wants their own space.

Commercial Rent

The name says everything. This type rents real estate to businesses. Businesses and startups would love to own space in a strategic location with high visibility. If you meet these criteria, your property has already been awarded half the deal. This property can be used to store your inventory, as well as your garage, for a business that needs it, or for your family's shop. As you can see, there are endless possibilities.

The best thing about commercial rent is that you have the right to demand more money for businesses because your property serves as a critical asset. You could also be a monopoly in your area if it is the best place for just a few businesses. That's a great opportunity to take advantage of it!

Both commercial and residential rentals can generate you huge incomes each month and year. These streams of income are likely to surpass your active income and multiply you wealth in just days.

Additionally, you have the option to rent spaces for residential or commercial uses. For example, if your farmhouse is a luxury property, you can rent it out frequently for family birthdays and formal corporate events.

The Out Of The Box Solution

Airbnb could use you as a business resource if you have an entire apartment that isn't being used or even a spare area in your home. Business associations are a good idea. Your home is more likely than a luxury hotel to appeal to tourists.

If your space is excellent, it's possible to work with Airbnb. This can make you a very lucrative host.

But, what happens if I don't have any property whatsoever?

As I mentioned earlier, even if there isn't a silver spoon or all the riches to rent property, this idea can still be used. Rent a garage, backyard, or room in your home and you will start with modest earnings. It will grow quickly and you will be able to buy more property and make money while you save.

Another option is to leverage your existing savings and buy a small apartment. The following is important information for those who are just beginning to buy and own property.

Buy a house and a living area that isn't too extravagant. You should be financially responsible and able to stay within your means. There are more stakes than money and you don't need to spend too much.

Do not borrow money to buy something you cannot afford. Refrain from considering loans and credit. To buy property is insane. It is best to start small, and take advantage of your savings, if you wish to purchase a space. Bootstrap your way to success, use the birds in hand and make do with what you have. But don't pay for costs that you don't know how to recover.

The best way to see the potential of passive income from real estate rental is through a sophisticated approach. The last tip is important to remember:

Be sure your property meets all requirements.

Dealing with potential residents or business owners about renting terms is fair and reasonable.

Offer good stuff. You should take good care of your home. Before you rent out your property, ensure it's at minimum painted, cleaned, and furnished.

You should do extensive research on your potential tenant before renting commercial property.

Renting Real Estate may be an appealing option for you if you want to make a side income or as a primary source of income.

2. Rent Your Car

This idea works best for people who don't use their car often and have a second car. Because of the pandemic, many people work from their homes, so your car won't be used as often. Turo lets you rent your car to others. You can rent out your car for well over $1,000 per monthly, which is a huge benefit to most car owners.

Turo makes it simple to rent your car (to someone reliable) through Turo. It's a great option to offset the true cost associated with owning a car. You can manage ongoing costs such routine maintenance as fuel prices, replacement parts and repairs. Turo can help you pay for your car's costs, as well as passive income.

Turo isn't just the app that lets people rent their car. There are also other apps that utilize the Turo peer to peer model. If you do a Google search on "car rental apps", this list will appear.

Kayak

Enterprise Rent-A-Car

Virtuo

Zipcar

Getaround

Hertz

It is important to note that most apps have specific eligibility requirements before allowing you to use their services. Turo US users have to show proof that their car is legal and registered in the US.

Other requirements apply such as age. Turo will not take cars older than 12 year old. Turo limits the mileage to 130,000 miles and won't take cars older than 12 years. The UK and some other countries require that you are at least 21 years old.

For more information on this matter, please contact Turo's staff.

1. Registering with Turo

Once you are certain that your car meets Turo and other app requirements, then you can start to list your vehicle. There will be a few steps but they are easy to follow. Users will be required to show their license and insurance information.

2. Write detailed descriptions and photos of high-quality

Turo needs you to take great photos that show your car. Turo even offers professional photographers who can come to your house to take photos. You can save money and do this yourself if you have the skills to use a camera.

Before you take pictures, make sure your exterior and interior are in perfect condition. A sunny day with good lighting is the best time to take photos using your cell phone. It is important to ensure that you have the lighting source behind the subject when taking photos. Otherwise you may overexpose.

Once you have excellent photos, it's now time to create detailed descriptions for the car. It's a rule of thumb that the more detailed the descriptions, the higher the response rate. Don't waste time writing long monologues. Simply cut to the essence and give the reader an accurate description of your vehicle. Detail the car's capabilities in rough terrain, Bluetooth connectivity, USB ports and fuel consumption.

Turo will help you get a general idea of what to talk about, so you won't be totally lost when you start writing descriptions.

3. You can set the right car rental price

For a rent price that attracts qualified leads to the listing, take into consideration the particular characteristics of your vehicle. It's not wise to guess at the price of your car. Instead, you can take a quick look at similar car listings to yours before setting a comparable pricing.

You might want to offer attractive discounts in order to attract more requests and clicks. The prices you set are not fixed. Demand curves and supply are constantly changing. Take the time to understand the current situation and adjust prices to make sure you are taking advantage of income opportunities.

Turo sends you a notification when someone rents your vehicle. However, to use the app, you will need to log into your account and agree to receive notifications. You can then have a chat with the person, and resolve any questions or concerns they may be about your car. This shouldn't take much time and shouldn't affect any other things you do throughout the day. Turo may take a small portion of your earnings (starting around 25%).

3. Start a YouTube Channel

YouTube launched the trend of passive income generation. YouTube remains one of the most rewarding websites on the web. PewDiePie, one of the most successful YouTubers, makes over $13M a year. That doesn't include sales from merchandise or sponsorships.

YouTube success can take a lot effort.

You can make a great living by learning the ropes and earning a steady paycheck each month. Your YouTube income can be passive as long the videos are being viewed after you upload them.

Signing up is the first step to create a YouTube channel. It's pretty self-explanatory. Once your YouTube account has been created, you will need the AdSense account to be linked to it. AdSense will be the main source for income for anyone just starting their business.

You will need to share important information such an employee ID number (EIN), social security number, and employer ID number (SSN) if your business is being run. AdSense is not always worth the money (and in some cases it is not even worth that much), however once you begin to generate attention on YouTube, your chances of securing lucrative deals and sponsorships will increase. You can also maximize your earnings with affiliate marketing. That's where you can generate real revenue. Your channel will likely grow and you may even be able, as many YouTube celebrities have done.

Making the Videos

Your video editing skills are your own. Although there aren't any set rules for success, it is clear that most of the most popular videos on YouTube were professionally produced. This means that you will need to have good video editing skills and expensive equipment. While it's possible to start recording using your phone, you won't get the same quality as professional video.

HD videos (720p would be fine) should be taken. A DSLR camera is best if you want the best quality. But potato quality will only take you so far.

Once you have obtained your footage it's time start editing it using Adobe Premiere Pro. YouTube does offer a basic video editor for free, but it is best to get past the steep learning curve using programs such as Adobe Premiere Pro. Another option is to hire a professional video editor (using platforms such as Fiverr and Freelancer), but this requires you to spend your money, which may not be possible for those just starting out.

When creating content for your YouTube channel, be careful not to use copyrighted materials (such as photos and music). This could render you ineligible at YouTube advertising.

Learn SEO for YouTube

Now that you have your video, it's now time to upload it onto the platform. Drag and drop your video directly into the uploader. Upload duration is dependent on the size and speed of your internet connection.

Once your uploaded video is uploaded, there will be an option to fill in the details. This is your chance optimizing your YouTube video for SEO. Change the title, description, tag, and other tags to reach a larger audience. You might also want to add hashtags (like Instagram and Twitter).

Promote Your Video

YouTube's algorithm can be difficult to understand, especially for beginners. It is a bit difficult to understand the YouTube algorithm, especially for beginners. We recommend sharing your video on blogs or forums and Reddit. It is important not to spam links on forums or blogs as it can lead to bans.

We do recommend learning YouTube Ads to help promote your content, if budget allows. This should help get you started with your viewership.

AdSense earns you a percentage of the total views and audience demographics. This can translate into higher earnings for Americans. You also get more clicks from advertisers.

It doesn't always lead to higher earnings, even though you have a large viewership. Engagement and clicks are essential. In fact, it is not uncommon for YouTube videos with more than one million views to make less money than those with just 100,000 views.

AdSense is not something you should rely on. Instead diversify your portfolio. Finally, analyze the performance to identify niches where you can prioritize video production. Your viewership and passive income will begin to grow quickly.

Chapter 10: Make extra money from freelancing platforms

Fiverr has been the best website I've ever worked for. Fiverr helped me make over $20000. I have never regretted opening my account on Fiverr. It has allowed me to meet some wonderful people and provided an opportunity for me to network with the best for some personal work.

Registering an account will allow you to offer services starting from $5. You can then add upsells or other packages to increase your order volume. Fiverr is a platform that allows anyone to make money, provided they have the drive and desire to satisfy their clients. You can offer services like writing, proofreading, book cover design, email marketing, etc.

HTTP://WWW.FIVERR.COM/

Upwork

Another great site for freelancing is Upwork. Like Fiverr you can earn a six-figure income in six months. Upwork makes it easy to create an account and start bidding on jobs that suit your needs.

If you're highly skilled, Upwork works well for you. While you might hear some negative comments about poor customers, intense competition, and the lack of raking in online cash, I still believe Upwork is a great option.

HTTPS://WWW.UPWORK.COM/

TopTal

Toptal, a global network of freelance software designers, developers, finance experts and product managers, is an independent network. Top companies hire Toptal freelancers in order to implement their most complex schemes. Toptal's remote work platform allows you to earn substantial money if your skills are in demand. Toptal gets thousands of applications every month. Typically, less than 3% are accepted.

HTTPS://WWW.TOPTAL.COM/

Free up

FreeUp allows you to earn anywhere from $15 to $30 an hour. You have to be extremely good at what it is you do to be accepted into the top 1%.

HTTPS://FREEUP.NET/

Superside

Join the UNIVERSAL Superside freelancers team to get paid to work for clients in your expertise. They provide a constant stream jobs on their website. There is no need for job hunting. The best part about their site is that they only hire the top 1% of global talent.

HTTPS://WWW.SUPERSIDE.COM/

It is necessary to

It's possible to earn up $50 per hour by working in a pinch. To make it happen, you just need to sign up for the marketplace, look for work, then have access and practical jobs in your specific area.

HTTPS://NEEDTO.COM/

Guru

Freelancer.com exists for a long period of time. It was something I worked for years before I switched over to Fiverr. PeoplePerHour in the United Kingdom is very common. These websites and those related to them all work and connect clients with freelancers.

HTTP://WWW.GURU.COM/

HTTPS://WWW.FREELANCER.COM/

HTTP://WWW.PEOPLEPERHOUR.COM/

Fancy Hands

Are you looking to work as virtual assistants? This platform is ideal for you. Fancy Hands allows you to become a virtual assistant on a US-based site. The best thing is that you are able to start working right away. This website is perfect for you, regardless of whether you are an assistant or want to do occasional tasks.

HTTP://WWW.FANCYHANDS.COM/

Zirtual

Do you want to be a virtual assistant or do you enjoy the idea of being one? This platform is great for you. Zirtual allows you to become a virtual assistant on their website. It is US-based. They train proactive and self-starter virtual assistants to excel at things that most people don't enjoy.

HTTPS://WWW.ZIRTUAL.COM/

Belay

Belay is another company that offers virtual assistant jobs. The hourly rate is typically between $10-$50.

HTTP://BELAYSOLUTIONS.COM/

Growth Geeks

This powerful, freelancing site was built by growth geeks to meet recurring monthly commitments. There will be gigs for Instagram and digital marketing. To have your service featured on the platform, apply to become a licensed Geek.

HTTPS://GROWTHGEEKS.COM/

Scribendi

Scribendi provides professional editors and proofreaders for remote work and client review.

HTTP://WWW.SCRIBENDI.COM/

Proofreading Services

Proofreading services is an English coaching and online proofreading company that's looking for individuals who can work from their home to teach English.

HTTP://PROOFREADINGSERVICES.COM/

Rev

Rev.com allows you the ability to convert Audio & Video files to text and earn as much as $1.25 per hour.

HTTPS://WWW.REV.COM/

ServiceScape

ServiceScape offers a freelance platform to professional writers, editors and translators. Simply register to begin working on this platform. Once you have the skill, you can earn money.

HTTPS://WWW.SERVICESCAPE.COM/

Chapter 11: Smart Investment Ideas

This has been a very informative article about passive income. However, there are still many options. This chapter will talk about exciting and new ways to increase passive income streams. These methods have been around for a long time, so let's take the time to look at them.

Rental Properties

Although it takes some effort to rent a home, you will reap the benefits in the long term. There is a large market for rental property. Some people, such a newlywed or college student, choose to rent over to buy at least initially. We all know that renters are not going to run out. There are many things to consider before purchasing a rental house. The market will be examined, the demand in your area will be determined, and you'll need to calculate whether rental properties will succeed in that area.

Why should you consider renting properties?

In the future, houses will be in great demand. With more babies being born every day, the number of people living in these houses is increasing. This number grows dramatically when you include immigrants. If you're lucky enough to find an area with high demand for rental housing, you might be in a golden spot. Renting out rental property is a great way to get rid of your principal loan. At first, rental income will cover both principal and interest. But as time goes on, only the principle will be paid, until that too is paid off completely.

An additional benefit is the fact that the IRS has decreed that renters will be exempt from tax. Because rental property has a fixed depreciation period, this benefit is also available. Depreciation refers to the fact that the property's usefulness is measured every year up until it has reached its end, after which it's no longer worth anything. Renters who own more than one property can have their tax liability reduced to nothing! This does nothing to reduce owners' cash flow but is used for income tax reporting. It is a real benefit that many rental property owners are able to reap the benefits.

The internet allows you to search for property without the need to speak to an agent. This will help you understand what to expect when purchasing rental property. This can be a good way to eliminate agents who are only interested showing you property they can't afford, that isn't in your preferred area, or simply not the right fit for your needs. I don't mean to discourage you from using an agent. But make sure that the agent knows what you want out of the prospective property. It is possible to avoid costly mistakes or overlook some important aspects of the rental process by working with an agent.

There are many benefits to renting out your rental property to you instead of paying someone to do it. You will feel that this is your business. This property will make you feel happy and proud, especially if you are the first to rent it. Why wouldn't you feel that way? It is a challenge to manage a rental property, but you won't be bored. There will always be something to do. Imagine the satisfaction that comes from knowing your tenants are happy and satisfied with the work you have done. It will save you money on fees if you do not pay someone else to manage the rental property. Instead, use the money for more productive purposes.

Technology has made managing rental properties much simpler than it was in the past thanks to computers and the internet. If you learn enough skills to manage your rental property, you may even be able offer your services as an extension of your own rental property management business and potentially make extra money. The majority of renting property is a profitable venture that will provide you with a steady stream income. There are many things you can do to ensure that your rental property is profitable. But we'll get to those methods later in the chapter.

How to get involved

First, it is essential to know what you want. This may also require you to train your mind and be disciplined. The goal is to purchase rental property. Although it can sometimes seem complicated or risky, it's possible to go in with an open mind. Clear thinking is essential if you want to avoid any pitfalls. If you are looking to buy rental property, you need to be able analyze deals. This requires you to develop your mathematical skills specific to your real-estate deal. By becoming an expert at analyzing the mathematical side of real estate deals, you will be able predict whether rental properties will generate sufficient profits.

Next is to start searching for rental properties. This is easy to do online. Once you have found the perfect property for your needs, you can search the internet for more information. With practice, you will be able analyze any rental property you come across. This skill is crucial for beginners. Next, you should contact a professional real-estate agent. You will now be able to decide what type of rental home you are interested in buying. Communicate your criteria to the real-estate agent. You should ask about a swimmingpool. Maybe a double garage. How many bedrooms, bathrooms and square footage should the property include? You can request that the agent send you emails when a property fits your criteria.

This is the time you need to find a lender so that you can get pre-approved. Once you are approved, you will be able to search for properties. Keep looking at potential properties. This will allow you to know how much the property will cost you. It will also help you to understand what you want from your rental property to make it a profitable investment. Make an offer when you spot property that has the right potential. You won't necessarily get accepted but make it a point to make at the least one offer each week. Keep looking at potential properties and keep making offers.

Accepting your offer means that you can now find suitable tenants. Interviews are the best way to select your tenants. During an interview, you can explain clearly what your agreement is, and what you expect them to do as tenants.

Don't let someone else rent your property because you are sorry. You'll need to be strict and look at the long-term advantages of having suitable tenants living in your rental home. Do as many interviews and as many questions you like. Your rental property should be able to generate passive income. If you pick the wrong tenants, your rental property could be a liability. Once your tenants have moved in, start to build a relationship. It is important not to invade their privacy with too many visits. As the property's owner, let them know that you're available for them when they need you.

Rental Properties to Ensure Steady Passive Income

Research is essential before purchasing any potential rental property. It is vital to consider the location. Property in areas with high unemployment is desirable. It is also important that you know the status of your current tenants. It is also important to understand the market for a particular area. It is important to research the cost of housing within the area you want to rent. This will give you an idea of the amount of rent you might be able charge.

Tenants who are happy will make your rental property more attractive to long-term tenants. If you have a maintenance problem, fix it right away. Avoid buying property in noisy areas. Many people prefer to live in quiet and peaceful areas. Be sure to show your tenants that you care. To resolve any problems your tenants may have, it is important to address them promptly. Multi-unit property owners should install laundry facilities to make life easier for their tenants. The best way to earn extra cash is to purchase commercial washers/dryers so that tenants do not have to travel to other places to wash their clothes.

If you are buying a rental property, do not go into debt. If the down payment cannot be provided by a business partner, ensure that it is money that's already yours. By doing this, passive income will be generated from the rental property. Once you own your first rental house, you will be able to purchase more. As your portfolio increases, you will be able to buy more and have a greater passive income stream.

By ensuring that the property appreciates, you can increase its value. This can be achieved by adding a bedroom, a bathroom, or increasing the garage's space. There are many methods to increase the value of your property and increase your passive income stream.

You could even build an addition building on the property that can house additional tenants. This will increase your passive income stream and the property's overall value.

Equity financing can be a better alternative to debt financing. Equity financing is when the loan used to finance a rental property is not considered a loan but an investment. Equity financing allows for greater flexibility than debt financing. You and the investor have several options for repaying the borrowed money.

Investing with Stocks

Most people now know what the Stock Market is. It is a place that allows you to buy and sell stock. Stocks are part ownership, which can be claimed on businesses. Stock prices can rise when there's a strong economy. Stock values fall when there is a weak economy. The reason stock can be sold by businesses is to make them more financially stable. Stock value will go up if the company is doing well. Sometimes, however the business may run into difficulties and then stock value can drop.

It is important that you understand the basics of the stock market. This is not an easy or risk-free way for you to become rich quickly. There are risks involved. You can't just blindly invest in stocks, hoping for success. When investing in stocks, you must take into account many factors. It is possible to reduce risks and earn more if your approach is smart.

Why should you consider investing in stocks?

Stocks are open to everyone. However, you cannot rely solely on luck when investing in stocks. The risks associated with investing will be minimized if you do your research. Ask any stock market investor and they will all agree that research is important. The internet makes it much easier for investors to invest in the stock exchange.

The more you explore the world of stock investment, the more you will gain. It might seem daunting at the beginning, but you will quickly realize that it is not. You can start investing using your smartphone. It doesn't really matter how much money or little you have. You can start investing with what you have. The best part about investing is that you don't have to work with a broker. It is possible to set up a brokerage on your smartphone and use it for investing in stocks.

If you are looking for financial security for your future, investing in the stock exchange can offer that. This is especially true for long-term investments. Your investments compound over time. For example, if you have invested money in the stock market for thirty years, it will grow exponentially. In return, you will be paid a healthy amount. As we discussed in Chapter 1, long term investments can also benefit your taxes. When the stock is sold, it will be regarded as a long-term capital loss. Many brokerages do not charge trading fees. This is because brokerages are like an online shop in which you can invest. This is great, especially if there's not a lot of money.

Every company that you purchase stock in is responsible for its growth. Stocks have many different options. You can be paid dividends. This means the company shares a portion of their profits with you. A second option is to sell stocks at a lower price than their original purchase price. This will result in a return on your investment. Inflation is on the rise every year so investing in stocks could help you beat it. Many tax incentives are available on the stock market.

Do not invest your entire capital in the stock markets if you do not intend to. Do not invest in the stock market with all of your money. It is a bad idea to take out a loan for investing. There are always risks associated with investing. You don't wish to put yourself at financial risk. However, if your stock market success is a good sign, and you have a solid passive income stream, it will allow you to buy more stocks and boost your income. Do not gamble on stocks. Stock investing is serious and requires research.

The best thing about stock market is the abundance of professionals available to help. It's easier than ever to keep up with all the latest stock markets statistics. This allows you to maximize your chances of making investing a success.

Marko of WhiteBoard Finance, 2020, believes that investing in stocks is the best and most efficient way to increase wealth. Stock market investments have an average annual return of 10%. Saving money isn't enough. Money loses purchasing power. It is possible to no longer buy the same things that you could five five years ago, if you find a $100 note in your closet. Because the $100 bill you found in your closet for five years has no purchase power. It has become more affordable to invest as many brokerages no longer charge trade fees. You have many options when buying stocks. These strategies can help you to be successful.

Chapter 12: Artificial Intelligence

your risk tolerance and goals. With no need to sell your investments, loans can be accessed at 2.50-3.75%. This represents a fraction the interest rates on credit cards and personal loans. Their AI can reduce the taxes that you have to pay.

How much will all this cost you? All you pay is a 0.25 percent annual advisory fee. No trading commissions. No sales calls. Seriously.

2) AI Trading Bots

You have two options to invest with bots. The first type of bots is those that study thousands upon thousands of stocks in order to make informed investment decisions. These robots could be used to automate your work and to make investments automatically. These are basically robo-advisors, which we have already mentioned.

The alternative, though more costly, is also more profitable. Trading bots are used to selectively invest with algorithms. Trading bots can be described as automated programs that connect directly to an exchange in order to trade on their behalf. They function using indicators and signals, including variations of moving averages. The benefits are significant when you have emotionless, 24/7 trading bots. Although trading robots have been around for a while by institutional investors they were only recently made available to everyone with an internet connection. Trading bots allow you to arbitrage across multiple cryptocurrency platforms. Quadency is one of the best platforms for trading bots. Quadency can be used as a trading platform to help you manage your crypto investments in any exchange.

Quadency is a professional trading platform for cryptocurrency assets. You can use it to install trading bots onto popular trading exchanges, such as Binance and Coinbase.

Quadency allows you access your entire portfolio via one interface. It also makes it easy to make trades. Quadency will allow you to manage crypto across multiple exchanges from one place. You do not need to log on to the exchanges.

From there, you can go on to the more costly bots which use the most advanced AI. Trade-Ideas remains the most popular platform. Trade Ideas cloud-based Artificial Intelligence market analysis platform. This powerful program has been backed by award-winning trading services. These services will allow you to capitalize on the ever-changing stock market. It covers many aspects of the financial marketplace.

Its A.I. Holly, the A.I. powered robot-adviser is made up of many investment algorithms. They are then subjected to millions trading scenarios nightly in order to select the most profitable subset for the next market session. Holly examines technical indicators, such as RSI/MACD/ADX, and even an AOI ("Automated optical inspection") of the prevailing trend to find optimal trades. It will also evaluate the market conditions, and all aspects of fundamental and social signals. The market will open, and the user will see the eight most profitable trading strategies, as well as the times to enter and leave these trades.

3) Hiring a Fiverr Developer To Create An AI App

Do you have an idea? A developer/coder is able to integrate artificial Intelligence to make your app even more useful. An AI app is soon to be released that can take a formal contract written in legalese and instantly convert it into a simple-to-read contract that anyone can understand.

For most people reading this, they are probably thinking "No way" that they can afford a developer. Nonsense. Use Fiverr. Fiverr offers a platform where you can create almost every type of product and service for just $5. The site offers services that allow you to hire anyone, anywhere in the world, to complete any task. Fiverr can help you find digital designers, web copywriters, or even app developers. A Bangladeshi developer won't charge you tenths of the Los Angeles fees.

4) Gambling Forecasts

AI is far better than humans at prediction, which is why they've been integrated into the financial industry at all levels. Bots can predict the weather, politics, and other events as well. A bot you can rent on Fiverr with the safest bets for blackjack. Then just let it go. This is a risky undertaking because you don't know the program's effectiveness. Similar to a stock trading program, you need to conduct your research and test the software to verify its effectiveness.

Intertops will allow you to start investing in long-term games if the basics of gaming are well understood. The robots allow you the opportunity to invest in roulette, craps, and blackjack. You'll see long-term gains. Blackjack is an example of a strategy where you can gradually build up your bankroll while becoming a solver. It is also worth looking at sports betting, horse racing, and card game like poker.

5) Create Art using AI

Imagine a world that AI can create art at a level never imagined. AI already does this. These are websites that combine AI and your imagination to create work of art that may just floor you: Artbreeder. The digital art you create can then be sold on innovative exchanges like Niftygateway. Digital art can sell for hundreds or thousands of dollars.

6) AI Solutions for Cash

This is one of most lucrative ways to utilize AI currently, especially for large companies like Google and Facebook. Collect as much data possible with AI models and then offer it to companies looking for profit. Companies and research groups are always in search of data to improve customer experience and be more competitive. It is best to concentrate on a narrow niche to limit competition.

Netflix uses AI to predict what your next viewing habits will be. However, did you know that they use this prediction in order to ensure that the content is available on the closest server near your location. This will ensure that this content plays smoothly, and with the highest quality possible. Netflix is able save money by not needing to store every series or movie on every server.

If you're looking for something more, you can even analyze the data and sell it to foundations and companies. This "AI solution" freelance job can be done through Fiverr.

7) AI ETFs are Exchange Traded Funds.

This would be the safest and most passive investment you can make with this list. An exchange traded mutual fund (ETF), which tracks an index, a commodities, or a portfolio of assets and is listed on a stock exchange, is an investment vehicle that tracks these items. For example, an ETF that tracks the top clean energy companies such as Tesla and Nio would be my investment. This way, I don't have the responsibility of selecting which companies I invest in. It's a similar investment as mutual funds, but you can buy and sell it just like stocks on an exchange. This allows investors to save money and keep track easily of their investments.

Investors seeking to ride the market waves can now find artificially intelligent ETFs. These algorithm-driven funds can be trusted to provide long-term security. Because they don't require live management, they are cheaper.

AIEQ, the most prominent of these AI ETFs, beat the S&P 500 last. IBM Watson powers AIEQ.

Newbies can benefit greatly from AI

Anyone starting to invest on traditional stock markets, I recommend that they use AI through robo advisors. These robo advisory companies are very well managed, as was mentioned earlier. Not only will they help you quickly learn, but you'll also be light years ahead the 95% who believe they can beat markets. As they are cheaper than traditional financial professionals, you will find that your money is saved a lot. These are also safer options if you're looking to invest large amounts. AI will help you make your money work harder.

Chapter 13: Other Ways To Increase Your Income

There are many other ways to increase revenue, in addition to the methods mentioned above to increase passive income. This chapter is for creative people who are both smart and creative. In addition to peer-to peer lending, we'll also be discussing how you can create online courses and sell them. Are you already excited?

Selling Courses

There are many courses online that have been popular recently. The courses range from financial and spiritual advice to how to keep a garden alive. There are thousands of courses that can be found on just about any topic. It is not hard to see why people are so in love with the internet. Search engines have made it possible for people to find information that was previously unavailable. Your knowledge can be shared worldwide if your creativity and intelligence are both strong. With the right knowledge, it is possible to create courses in your specific area of expertise that will help educate the entire world. Now you can put all your knowledge to good use. You can finally unleash the genius in you and be creative!

Why Should You Consider Selling Courses?

You remember the time as a kid when you had to go to the library to find all the information needed for a school project. Today, all it takes to find the same information is a click away. The internet has made knowledge easier. This is why you should put your knowledge to work and gain benefits. It will benefit not only you, it will also benefit others.

It's possible to sell online courses, and create a passive income stream by creating them. You can sell your courses online and make a great passive income stream. Online courses are easy to create and sell.

Online courses are used by bloggers, YouTubers, podcasters and others to boost their revenues. To increase their revenue, experts are creating online classes. If you are an expert in a particular field, you can also create online courses and make them available online. Additionally, many aspects of your field of interest are interrelated. You can create multiple courses covering different topics and thus create an even more passive income stream. If you own a business, an online course could be created that will direct clients to your site and help them buy the products or services you offer. Your customers will be able to benefit from the course, especially when your product requires some knowledge. This type online course can increase awareness of your business, product, or cause, as well as your profit.

Online courses can not only increase passive income, nor the knowledge and skills of the purchasers, but also serve to transform lives. Although creating an instructional course may require some effort and time, the maintenance and marketing of it will be much easier. There's a market for online classes because people are eager to learn more and get better at what they love. Many young people don't have the financial means to pay for college, so they choose online courses. They save money by learning online. Additionally, they can work at their own pace and from their home. It is possible to develop intuitive, interactive intelligence using technology.

Many people don't realize how much they have been hiding. You may be one of those people. This knowledge cannot be shared with friends or loved ones, so it's best to keep your mouth shut while the valuable knowledge swirls around in you brain. All that is left! There are people around the world who are open to your knowledge. I'm sure of that. A course online is the best way to go about it. If you are unsure about whether there will be an audience for your course, you could allow people to prepurchase the course. This will give your a better idea of how many people are interested in the course and if it will be worthwhile. Potential students will also be able inform you about their learning needs and help you adjust the course to fit them.

With this information in mind, let us move to the next part. Here, we will talk about selling your course online.

How to sell online courses

You will first need to select the topic for your course. Your knowledge is vast and you have many things to consider. Find an aspect that can be transformed into a meaningful, educational, and fun course. The topic you choose should not be considered passive income. However, it might create passive income streams if people aren't interested in it. A survey can be sent to potential students as a way to help you determine the topic. This can be done using a website like Typeform. You can then see what areas need your expertise. Facebook can be used for surveys.

Once you have selected the topic, you need to develop your course. This will allow you to have a clearer picture of what you are looking for in your course. Think about starting at the bottom and moving to the top. This can help to create a course that has a balanced flow. Decide what you want to teach your students and what you want them learning at the end. You can work around this by deciding which steps must take before reaching milestones. You can always remove anything from this course that you feel is unnecessary. You may wish to keep it aside for future reference.

Once you're done, it's time to start working on the actual course. As visual aids, your course can contain pictures, videos, or both. Visual stimuli can be positive for people, so it will make your course more successful. Consider adding quizzes to your course. Make your course as interactive and engaging as possible. Avoid unnecessary fluff. Be clear about the purpose of your course. It is important that your students understand the main points. These key points are what you should be focusing on. Make sure your students succeed by following your online courses. This is why they are interested in your course.

The course will determine which type of material and camera equipment you will use. If you're presenting a course in finances, then you won't need a full body shot. Students will see your face on the screen, while the rest of it is for demonstration purposes. Filming your course, say, on football, will require you to film the whole person or group differently. Now it's time for you to host the course.

You should consider self-hosting. But you will still need to take care of everything. A website, payment processing software, as well renting a server will all need to be purchased. You'll be responsible for any technical issues. Your website may crash if it receives too much traffic. Udemy is another option. They do most of your work so it might sound appealing. They determine everything including what price you can charge and how payment plans will be made. They will also manage your communication with students.

There's also a third option: learning management platforms like Thinkific. All you need to do is create an online account, upload your course and set up your payment plans. Then, host your course! It is very easy yet very effective. With an intuitive interface and all the tools necessary, you will be provided with everything you need. For pricing to be fair, you'll need to do market research.

Peer-to -Peer Lending: A Strong Passive Income Source

Before you decide to invest, you can research a few things about the borrower. It would be safer for younger people to invest in those who work in an office environment. There is no risk of serious injury in an office environment. However, young people who are borrowers or working have a good future.

Also, young people are less likely to develop health problems.

If you're interested investing in short-term loan, you don't need to wait too much to see your return. The interest rates on this type of loan can also be very high because it is often given to borrowers in extreme need. Although it might be appealing to invest in an unregulated loan platform, the risks involved can be very high. It is better that you stick to the trusted and regulated peer to peer lending platforms. Consider that you will not receive monthly payments on a longer-term loan. On the other hand, consumer loans will provide you with a monthly payment. The risk is lower for both the principal and the interest.

Keep in mind that there is a second type of peer-to–peer platform. The first is peer-to–peer loan marketplace. This platform does not lend money out to borrowers. However, it can be used to help fund loans by different lending firms. The marketplace acts as the link between the borrower's peer-to–peer lending platform, and the marketplace. This can be used to expand your portfolio because the marketplace lists more loans that the platform. Peer-to-peer loans are the second platform. The peer-to-peer loan platform connects you directly to the borrower.

In order to have a steady stream of passive income, you must find the best peer-to–peer lending platform. Do your research to determine the best platform for you. P2P Empire can help you compare the different platforms to determine which one suits your needs. Check which platform has the highest loan availability. It is possible to test out a platform by investing a small amount into one loan. See what the interest rate on the particular platform is. It is important that you only invest on a properly regulated platform. This protects investors from any potential scams. Check out the return rate and the number investors to gauge how popular the platform.

Most platforms have a blog you can check out. Don't be surprised if there are no statistics or numbers posted on the blog. The blog should contain information about the platform, its partners, not random information which may be irrelevant. You may also need to investigate the platform's owners and CEOs, as some could be guilty of financial misconduct. Before you sign up, make sure to read and comprehend all terms. While many people opt to skip this step, it could mean that your money is at risk. Take the time to carefully read the agreement. Keep in mind that fees could also be mentioned within the terms. If you didn't read them, it would be difficult to know about such fees. During an investigation, you may include financial information on platforms. You'll be able to determine whether the platform is viable.

Chapter 14: How to Make Passive Income

AIRBNB RENTING OUT PROPERTY

Are you going to be away on the weekend? It's a good idea to have someone stay at the house while you're away. Airbnb has revolutionized the rental industry. Many tourists prefer to stay at a house instead of a hotel. To fund your vacation, it is sensible to generate passive income. It's possible to rent your property out to people who are attending a major local event like a festival, college football game, or other significant events.

Airbnb is an excellent way to make passive income from a property you own, particularly if it's located in a tourist area. Since you won't be using it all year, there are more opportunities to rent it out. If you let more people rent your property, you might be able to make more money without disrupting the normal flow of your life.

Did you realize that homeowners can rent out their homes via AirBnb to earn up $10,000 per month? (Source). Isn't this amazing? You don't even have to spend much time or money to generate passive income. Continue reading if there is a property you want to rent out with this popular service.

Is it possible with AirBnB to earn passive income by renting your home? AirBnB allows you to rent your property and make passive income. This service is increasingly popular with travelers who prefer to rent a homestay over a hotel when travelling around the world. AirBnB is a passive revenue source that automates and outsources the renting process.

Based on estimates, around half of AirBnB tenants earn at most $500 each month. Here's how you can figure out how much you might earn on AirBnB each year. For four people staying in Boston, our budget was $25,000 This revenue can be earned passively without any investment. It can become quite a task if you don't pay attention.

What are the advantages of AirBnB?

AirBnB has many similarities to other peer market services. Instead of selling your home or crafting products online, you can rent your couch, room or entire house out on AirBnB. Airbnb has quickly become a preferred choice for people looking for a place to stay when they are planning their next trip.

Airbnb is an online platform that has been around for a while but has recently emerged as a viable alternative to local hotels. AirBnB is a platform that provides international exposure for hosts, insurance, assistance, feedback, and feedback.

AirBnB Passive Income: Rent your Home to Make a Passive Living

AirBnb allows guest to rent out their home for a modest fee. AirBnB lets you rent your home or room to guests for a small commission. Here's how it works passively.

1. AirBnB Rentals: Get Ready

It must be accessible for all guests who wish to stay in your house or apartment. It must offer clean, well-furnished spaces and essential facilities like power and water. Access to basic necessities such as electricity, parking, internet, and bedding (soft or firm) is essential. The basics include soap, towels, and toilet papers.

Be sure to properly photograph your place. AirBnB is available to assist you with professional photography or to hire a professional photographer if your skills are not up to the task. Photos are the biggest selling point of an AirBnB listing. You should inform neighbors about visitors arriving and departing as you prepare your house. Finally, you must clean your home of all clutter.

2. Understanding Your Target Market

Every home is unique. Each one appeals to a specific set of tenants. A huge property in a city will not attract the exact same clientele as a small cottage. It is important that you choose a home to rent to tenants who are compatible with your goals. You need to research what kind of renters your home is likely to attract. Some tenants may require more amenities than others. For more information, look at comparable ads in your local area and read reviews from previous customers.

3. Posting your Listing

Sign up whenever you're ready for an AirBnB listing submission. The AirBnB website can be accessed easily and is highly user-friendly. Personal information will include your name and contact information. A description of your house and photos of your space will also be needed. You can add house rules to your description that your tenants will have to follow while living in the home. You can restrict the number of people who can stay in your home, or create cancellation policies.

AirBnB has an automatic tool that will help you to find the right price for you home.

AirBnB will automatically determine how long you'll be staying at your house each night if that option is chosen.

4. Screening your guests

AirBnB may not be able to rent your house to everyone. You may have neighbors who are concerned about your guests throwing parties at your house. Screening potential guests before you list your house is a good idea. Check out their previous comments before accepting a request from a renter.

AirBnB is the best-known site for short-term rentals. There are many other sites that offer peer to peer rentals. Here are some tips to help you choose the right AirBnB rental room.

Advertise your house correctly by listing all the necessary amenities, in addition to the usual home features that guests would expect. Be sure to surprise your guests with small touches that will make their stay even more enjoyable. A welcome box with chocolates, wine, chocolates, and other small touches can encourage guests to return. They may even leave positive comments about your listing. Your listing's photos could make or break you. You should upload photos of your house that are clear and good quality.

AirBnB requires a host to pay a fee of 3% on all bookings. The guest will also be charged a commission ranging from 6% to 12%. Make sure you take the time and learn about the local tax rules for renting your property. AirBnB services are available around the globe. Each country will have its own rules and regulations for dealing with tax authorities. A tax professional can provide additional information.

How passive is AirBnB rental?

Renting out houses is a passive way of making money. AirBnB is a passive way to make money. It depends on how active you are. These are some of the things you can do in order to make this as passive as possible.

If you rent out large areas, consider installing a keypad or self-locking mechanism. They can check-in or leave themselves, making it much easier for you.

Hire a service for cleaning: A cleaner should come to your house and clean up after guests have left. They should change the bedding, and make sure that everything remains in excellent condition. If they notice anything that is missing, damaged or requires reporting, let them know.

A hired assistant can help you make this process easier. Let them have a piece of the listing so that they can manage guest inquiries, vetting potential tenants and other problems. They can also update the listing and make comments to tenants.

AirBnB makes it easy to rent your house. If you think about how much you can make from this company, this is one of your best options to supplement income. It could turn into a fulltime job if the tasks you perform are all yours.

Scalability

AirBnB allows you to rent out one property, which isn't feasible for most people. Renting additional properties can help you grow your business. A single property, in a great area, can make you a lot. Additionally, you have the option to grow the company by increasing how often you rent it. You can learn more about your monthly revenue potential for AirBnB within your area by using the tool on AirBnB.

Startup costs

This is a great company to start as there is no capital investment. You can go as long you have one or more spare rooms. It is enough to place your ad on the internet so potential tenants can find you. It is possible to invest money in your home, or make improvements to your listing. However, it is not necessary for those who already own a clean, neat place. AirBnB charges a host fee to rent your space.

Difficulty

AirBnB makes it simple to rent your property. If you have a house to rent, and are willing to list it on the site. If you use the following basic principles, you shouldn't have any trouble advertising your house or making passive income.

Time

The most time-consuming task is to create your listing and take high-quality photos at the beginning. It is possible to outsource your job and rent your property, but it will take less time. The majority (if not all) of the ongoing labor involves cleaning, washing, or interacting with tenants or potential guests. With a padlock, check-in or checkout can be automated. The task can then be delegated to an assistant for cleaning and maintenance.

Risk

AirBnB rental of your property can pose serious risks, especially when you have no control over the tenants. You may end up giving your listing away to unsavory people. It is possible to reduce this risk by refining how you choose tenants and ensuring that applicants are screened prior to accepting your requests.

Seasonality

AirBnB renting is seasonal, depending on where your home is located. It is possible that your business will not be affected by seasonality if it is located in an area that has a high level of tourists. If there is a seasonal spike in tourists in certain parts of the year, it is possible to expect some seasonality.

Return on Investment

AirBnB is a great place to rent your home. The reason is that it costs very little to advertise your house and all you need to offer your visitors is free. This passive business will bring you a high rate of return on investment.

Chapter 15: Habits and The Brain

We create our habits first. Then our habits make ourselves." - John Dryden

People often say things like "I should wake early" or "I should set goals every day and prioritize my tasks," or "I should stop wasting time and not spend too much", or "I should exercise more regularly and meditate to concentrate better." It is common for women to desire to improve their lives. They can also do this by following good habits that many successful women are doing. Good habits are vital for both personal and professional success. Good habits not just help with success, but also allow you to live a happier and more productive life. Many of you may wonder if it's possible to change bad habits and achieve success. Numerous studies supporting the connection between habits of success and success show that around 40% of all actions taken by people every day are actually behaviors and not just decisions.

Here you'll find out the importance and methods of developing good habits. Have a glance.

Good Habits: How Important Are They?

Habit is an activity that a person regularly does without conscious thought. Your success or failure depends on what habits you have. Humans are the only creatures that have the ability to change bad habits and adopt the one that works better. The brain loves to automate the process of creating a routine. The brain enjoys automating a sequence of steps to create a routine. This gives it enough time for other processes that are related to making decisions. Habits not just get stronger with each day, they also have the tendency to become automatic.

The brain begins to respond to a woman following a schedule. Good habits are what will determine a woman's growth and development. A woman can be successful and happy, regardless of her bad habits.

A woman can achieve success with certain good habits, such as regular exercise, meditating and challenging herself. You will be glad that you can create the life you want. Every kind of habit can help you accomplish any goal that you set in a given time frame. You cannot start or buy a handmade decor store through social media. Set a goal of finishing twenty to thirty bottle painting within the first 24 hours. This does not mean you can't reach your goal. This particular goal might take some time. It is essential that you have a consistent habit of painting your bottles as fast as possible. This will help you reach your goal. One day you'll be able finish your goal of customizing 30 bottles or painting them all in one day. It is essential to develop good habits, such as being goal-oriented, in order to live a disciplined and better life.

Another important aspect of good habits is their ability to set a solid foundation for life. When choosing which habits to adopt, be cautious. This is because your lifestyle choices can set the tone of your entire life. If you enjoy exchanging smiles with people, and if your smile brightens someone's day then you will be remembered as a happy lady. To the contrary, a healthy lifestyle that involves eating one boiled veggie with each meal will help you be a person who puts her health first. A good habit for any woman who is successful is to be mentally and physically healthy. It can help you succeed in your professional life.

Poor habits can also be used to reduce wasted time. The majority of human beings have a tendency for wasting time. This can be done by sitting idle, thinking about insignificant ideas, or simply daydreaming. A majority of people are not prepared to take on any difficult or challenging task. If you are prepared to do difficult work, you will be able to feel the thrill of success. If a person has good habits and practices them, they can be more efficient and less likely to waste time. The result is that wasted time can become productive.

Also, good habits can replace motivation. People experience times when they feel like giving up on their goals, getting things done, or eating right. The best thing is to make these things your routine and you will do them without a second thought. Let's say that gratitude, or writing down ten- to twelve things each day is your routine. If you are feeling down, you might just want to give up on this habit. Out of regular practice, however, you will still be able to write at least two to three entries on your diary. You'll be more energetic the next morning and have the energy to carry on the habit. So, good habits can help a woman reach any goal and accomplish any plan. Habits are constant and essential for success.

Develop Good Habits

Now that you know the basics of good habits, it is possible to discover strategies and ways to help you develop and keep those good habits. You will find that changing habits or developing new ones is not an easy or quick process. It can also be quite difficult. To develop effective habits, patience, discipline, persistence and perseverance are key factors.

First, get rid of negative beliefs. Don't feel discouraged if something goes wrong at your workplace or home. It doesn't matter if it's a single mistake. It doesn't mean you have to pick up a new habit every single day. One person is never perfect. If you happen to miss practicing your newly acquired habit one day, it is okay to do so again the next day. The key ingredient to being positive when trying to establish any good habits is optimism. Positive thinking will help you overcome any negative feelings. It will also give you the strength to cope with stressful situations. Positivity is one of your best tools to help you develop better habits. This does not mean that everything must be ignored and you must continue your daily tasks. It's important to find positive ways to deal with unpleasant situations. If your thoughts about changing any of the habits you have are negative, it will be extremely difficult to implement it.

A clear understanding of the triggers, obstacles, and other factors that can hinder your ability to create a habit is crucial for any successful one. Without identifying all of these factors, you might not be able to successfully adopt the habit. It is possible that you will encounter some difficulties when you are trying to change your habits. However, those bad days can be overcome by not returning to old bad habits. If you do, all your efforts to rid yourself of bad habits will go sour. You can instead try to do something productive. It will help reduce stress levels and also make you feel more positive.

The next step is to take some time and reflect on the reasons you are unable to practice a good habit. This will help you find the best solution for your problems. Plan for success with failure in mind. Although you are working to adopt a positive habit, it is not possible to expect success within a couple of days. The truth is that failures are possible before you can become accustomed to the new habits. If you are positive about your failure and don't think about quitting, your chances of creating a better habit will be slim. Instead of feeling guilty or giving in, create a plan. This will help you get back on track quickly. There is no difference between individuals who break a good habit or those who do not. All that matters is having a solid plan to handle failure.

Celebrate small wins. This is a common strategy that most successful women follow to get more. As an example, let's suppose that you smoke approximately ten cigarettes each day and you are trying hard to quit. You cannot expect to stop smoking entirely the moment you decide to quit. It is a small win to smoke just four to five cigarettes a day after you quit. If you do this, you will feel motivated to create a better future. You have to be patient and realize that developing a positive habit takes time. The goal should be to only make 1% of the improvement. For small successes, reward yourself with something of your choosing to stimulate your brain's reward network. Also, small steps that are successful can be rewarded and celebrated to help you feel more confident in your ability make anything possible.

If you want to build a good habit fast, it is possible to break it into small steps. You then can concentrate on one step at once. It is one the best methods to maintain consistency. To the contrary, you should shift your thoughts from the past habit and put more focus on the ones ahead. Prior to making the decision to incorporate a healthy habit into your daily life, you need to be clear on the reasons why. It is crucial to reflect on why this habit is important for you, as well as how it will help your achieve your goals. There is a possibility that your mind is unclear and you might feel stressed.

If you want to incorporate a good habit, the first thing is to stop judging others and underestimating them. Instead of being negative about yourself, keep an attitude of "Yes, I can do it!" This attitude will help you be more motivated to make a habit.

Get rid of bad habits

Habits that hinder your growth and development are the main reason you don't reach your goals. They not only put your health in danger, but also make it difficult to use your time and energy effectively. Don't worry! You can kick this bad habit by following these simple steps.

To eliminate a bad habit, you must first identify the behavior you wish to change. Next, you must choose a new bad habit. Prepare a plan before you feel the urge to relapse to your bad habit. As an example, suppose that you are trying to quit smoking and have the urge to start. What are you going to do? You might plan to do breathing exercises whenever you feel the need.

You must eliminate your triggers as soon as possible. If you have a bad habit of smoking cigarettes, alcohol might be a trigger. It is better if you stop drinking alcohol or going to bars. By avoiding doing the tasks that cause bad habits, you can make it easier for yourself to eliminate them. Your environment plays an important role in making good habits easier and bad habits harder. It is possible to change your environment and get rid off bad habits. This will help you change the overall outcome. Bad habits can be eliminated by being patient and kind with oneself. You may now know that changing bad habits and adopting good ones takes time. It is important to learn how to manage your frustrations and temper, even if the process takes a little longer. Your brain needs some time to create new connections and let new patterns in behavior.

Staying in touch will help you to avoid ill-health habits. However, this does not mean that all of your former friends should be abandoned or forgotten. It is possible that you will find new friends with the same goals or targets as you. Visualize your success. Visualize breaking whatever bad habit it is that you are trying to overcome. If you find it difficult to quit bad habits, you can seek professional help.

Chapter 16: Selling Stock photos

Are you a shutterbug? Are you a photographer? Are you naturally skilled at taking perfect photos?

So why not make a living from your skills?

Your photo-taking addiction can be turned into passive income. You can sell your photos online. There are many websites that pay for every photo you download.

Each one of these online photo-selling portals has a different pricing structure. However, these online photo selling sites are a great way for hobbyists to generate passive income. Edit and upload your photos once. Then, every time someone downloads, or purchases, your photo is royalty-free.

Here are some quick tips to help you find the best websites for earning with your photographs.

500px Prime

This website has over 5,000,000 photographers. You will receive 70% of each sold license. A standard license can be purchased for $250. Images that are commercially licensed may be bought by big brands.

To create a store, sign up for free, submit your images, and enable it. Next, complete the form for each of your images.

SmugMug Pro

This will allow you an 85 percent markup on every image sold. The downside is that you cannot get a free membership. Instead, you'll need to subscribe to the "Pro" plan, which costs $12.50 each month.

After creating an account you will upload photos and choose which images you want for sale. SmugMug Pros may be the right place to start if entrepreneurial thinking is your thing.

Shutterstock

Shutterstock can pay up to $120 per image. The pricing structure for this portal can be quite complex but you can make a good amount of passive revenue. Shutterstock's images have been downloaded more than 500,000,000 times, and the collective earnings of photographers exceed $300 million.

You can also sell images, vectors, and stock clips in HD and 4K resolutions on this website. You can also earn money by referring other photographers. You usually earn 4 percent per image they sell.

Referring customers that purchase images from you will get 20 per cent commission. A cap of $200 is allowed.

iStockphoto

iStockphoto started in 2001. They have a large network with image contributors. The service also checks applicants thoroughly to ensure they are a good fit in their community.

Fill out the application form if you are interested in applying.

The iStockphoto review will take place to verify your qualifications. They then ask for you to take a brief assessment quiz. If you are selected, you will be asked for a couple of samples to ensure your work meets the highest standards.

You would begin to receive at least 15 percent on every sale once you have been accepted. But, if accepted, you will receive a minimum of 15 percent on each sale.

Chapter 17: Self-Publishing

In this chapter, we will look at the entire self-publishing project. Each step will be examined and we'll show you how to make it passive.

Self-publishing allows you to print your book by waiting for a customer to order.

This is an interesting model since it doesn't force us to print hundreds or distribute them to libraries in hopes of sales. We will not incur additional costs for book production and will not have any unsold stock.

The book can be written by you personally or by a ghostwriter. As you never have to worry about books being sold, this allows you to infinitely multiply the work.

Let's go over the stages of the entire process:

PHASE 1, Research

The research phase follows the ones that were previously examined. We want to find a niche in which we can sell books. However, there is very little competition. If the niche does NOT meet these requirements it will be necessary to change it or work in a secondary related niche.

Once the niche is identified, we will work the same way on the main keywords, analysing the results.

The software allows you to analyse the keywords manually or automatically. You can manually search Amazon by entering your keywords and then analyzing the results. Checking if the books are selling properly, looking for competitors and if there is a self-publisher, we will need to do this.

This is important because if publishers are our competitors, it means that our battle has already been lost. If self-publishers are our competitors, we will only need verification that the book has been there for a long duration and that they have not had many reviews. If the keyword is intriguing, the search result will result with good selling books and no less than two or three strong competitors.

The use of software to perform keyword searches can reduce time and increase efficiency. Softwares products like Kdpspy Rocket Publisher, Helium10 and Helium10 are great research partners.

We will just need to insert the keyword. Then, we'll get all the details, such as reviews and sales figures, for the best books.

We can also export our searches to be later imported, analyzed and all this with just a few mouse clicks.

PHASE 2. Book creation and distribution

Now that we have identified the niche and created the keywords for the product, we need to make it. Our product is a novel. The first stages of its creation will include the content writing process and the cover creation.

A. Content writing

The basic idea of the content is what guides the writing process. As a top-down method, we will refine the idea. Next, we will create the topic scheme and then move to the structure.

Keep it casual and friendly. Avoid complicated language forms. A professional can review the form if you are unsure. You don't have to worry about how much it will cost. However, increasing the quality of your sales will bring more customers.

Grammarly is a program that allows you to inspect your grammar. It can detect punctuation and errors in grammar.

If you pay someone to write it, ensure that you always improve the quality of your content.

Writing books can be an integral part of your business. It is important to have the process outsourced to companies or freelancers. This allows for you to focus on your business and save time on all other aspects. Unfortunately, not all writing companies work well, especially if you rely on cheap ones. It is essential to control both form and content, as it can lead to plagiarism.

Formatting text, is another important aspect.

There are ready-to–use templates available for these editors: while they are relatively simple models, their results won't be as professional or as those produced by commercial software such as Scrivener, Ulysses and Indesign.

The same styles should be used for each section (titles, subtitles, and text bodies) and fonts with a standard size are often used (e.g. 12, 12).

B. B.

The cover should reflect your niche. I recommend that you study the covers that have sold well in your niche. It's possible to find out what makes those books stand out. These examples can be used to help you create your own.

Although you can create your book's cover yourself, if not an expert or a graphic designer, it might be worth paying someone to do it. Beautiful covers can be made by professionals for a few hundred dollars.

C. Description

The description of the book should be as important than the cover. Customers will be attracted to a well-written description and this can result in increased sales.

You should highlight the things that make your book unique, or how it can help with particular problems. Also, you should compile a list of key points. Your book will have a better visibility if you include all keywords you found in the search phase.

D.

Amazon handles the loading of your book. Simply enter all information about the book, keywords, and then upload your manuscript and cover. The system will inspect the files and determine if there are any errors.

After uploading, the project will move to Amazon's final ratings. If no problems are found, your book is available online within 48-hours.

PHASE3 - Marketing

Amazon marketing serves only one purpose. This is to allow your product, in this case a ebook, to be featured on the first page for a particular keyword. The following are the main reasons why your book might appear on this particular page:

A) Amazon customer ordered your book after conducting a search for certain keywords.

Amazon recognizes that you have increased sales and gives your product a greater importance in related searches. The reason is simple: Amazon algorithms detect your product being purchased often every time a keyword keyword is searched. As a result, your product will appear more often in search results.

B. Amazon Ads displays your book first on a page that is relevant to a particular keyword. In correspondence to certain areas that can be structured and designed with advertising messages, This is an excellent way to "push", sales and attempt to trigger point A. Everything is based around the auction mechanism. First, you set the price at which you would like to appear on page one. Then you join other competitors in an auction to bid for the most space.

Amazon Ads is extremely powerful for many reasons.

1) Prices are lower compared to similar advertising platforms (Google Ads & Facebook Ads).

2) Your target market is extremely targeted. Amazon shoppers are looking for items to buy. If your product is visible within the ad area of Amazon, it is likely that you will sell.

PHASE 4: Automate

Each step can be automated by software or a Virtual assistant.

The whole process can be automated by commercial software that facilitates keyword searching. Kdpspy Rocket publishers, Helium10, and Helium10, are some of the best and most reliable.

They all come from the commercial sector, but they enable us to automate this process quickly and in a valid way.

As mentioned above, you can automate the writing and creation part of your cover using writing companies or freelancers. But be sure to review the results.

The Marketing phase can be outsourced. For ads, we can use all the keywords from the indicated software.

PHASE 5 - Scale up

After we have established a team to do the various tasks, it will be easier to move up in the business. As supervisors, we will be able quickly to increase the number and quality of books that are published.

Chapter 18: Rental Property Investing

Cost: 4 Difficulty: 3 Risk: 4

As the market continues to evolve, you may be drawn to rental properties because of new trends in earning an income.

This data shows that investors have positive and promising prospects for investing in real estate. You will be more engaged with it. For those who are willing to take the risk, there is more information available. It will all be worthwhile.

Many novice property investors don't have the basic knowledge to purchase and invest in rental homes. They don't understand the industry and just start investing. This leads to failure. Before they know it, the money that they invested was already a waste. This is why you need to be clear about the fact that investing in rental properties can be a serious business decision.

You have the opportunity to become the next successful real-estate investor and make a wonderful passive income this year. Before you decide to take this risk, it is important that you assess your willingness and ability to accept it.

Rental Properties for Passive Income

Mashvisor reports that rental properties can be one of the best passive investments in passive income today for a variety of reasons. Here are some more:

Reason #1 - You'll get Rental Income

Rental properties are a great option because they can provide steady income. Imagine receiving a monthly rental check as payment. Like any product, you need to be careful about the quality. Renting a rental home is a good investment.

There are two types in real estate. The first are positively geared property, while the second are negatively geared. How does each differ from the others? Property with a positive gearing is one that generates cash flow. Conversely, properties with a negative gearing do not. This is why you should start with the first one if your goal is to become an expert in real estate investment.

Use the rental property estimator to help you ensure you're getting the best deals. It is a real-estate analytics tool that can greatly assist in property selection. You can also do a rental market analysis to better understand real-estate properties. The analysis includes the calculation both of the cash-on-cash return cap and rental revenue. This analysis will help you determine if it is worth taking the chance on a property. This tool can also be used to determine the profits and losses of a specific rental property.

Reason #2 - You do not get fully involved

Wow! This is passive income. It allows you to earn money while working less, or while you still have time for other activities. You can have a full time job while still earning income from your rental property.

You can benefit from property management to make smart investments. A professional company will manage all aspects of managing your property. These could include managing tenants, collecting rent in time and maintaining records. In the event of any issues, they can also manage legal matters related to your rental properties.

Real estate investing has become more appealing to you. However, property management service fees may be an additional cost. Be prepared for these fees. Add these charges to your budget.

#3 Reason: You Can Invest Part Time

You can make income with rental properties by part-time investing. This means you can keep your job of eight to five while still investing in your rental property. It's a convenient way to earn passive income.

Many people have made positive changes in their lives by renting property. Once you find the perfect property to invest in, you'll be glad for all the benefits you get.

#4: Investing Outside of State

A second way to invest in is becoming increasingly popular. It's out-of-state investing. When you're certain that the location is right for you, find it and purchase it. Short-term rentals such Airbnb rentals may be an option. This is a very lucrative way to invest. It is easy to locate the best Airbnb locations, review them, and then get rental fees.

There are many ways to make passive income from renting properties

Diverse methods can be used to generate passive revenue from real estate. Renting a rental property is a good investment strategy, which increases its profitability over the long-term.

Start a rental house in your community.

Take advantage of the opportunity to invest in your area.

Eliminate money pits. Don't be tempted into bargains.

To pay a smaller down payment, you will be making a greater investment.

Locate your rental property near schools in high demand.

Renting out rooms is a better way to make money than getting tenants who want to occupy the entire house.

You can decide the location based upon the property listings.

You can advertise your rental property on the best platforms

If you already own rental property, you have many options for how to market it. These are 25 places where your rental property can be promoted, according to PropertyWare.

Add some SEO to your Website

If your website is already online, you can promote your rental properties via a blog or a specific landing site. SEO strategies should be used to enhance your site's social media visibility.

Craigslist

Craigslist has become the leading platform for searching property listings. There is no cost to post on Craigslist. You can also create your own caption and upload photos.

Oodle

Oodle also offers a classified listing platform to rent rental housing. This site is not just a listing platform for property-related listings. However, it helps renters to locate the property they are searching.

Zillow

Zillow allows you add an interactive map, photo listings, as well as the ability to organize your search by bathroom, bedroom, or rental price.

Hotpads

This website allows users to list their unit or family buildings. It is also available for pet owners, as long as the website contains accurate information about their pets.

RentalHouses

The platform allows property owners and managers the ability to post their rentals, allowing them to be accessed in just a few seconds.

Realtor

This website sells rental properties and manages real estate. It allows property owners and property managers the ability to list their properties. It allows you to search by price or location.

Padmapper

This is a fun and interactive platform that allows renters set prices and bedrooms.

Trulia

This simple platform allows renters to set parameters for viewing a list of photo listings as well as other data about a property.

Simply stunning

It uses a simple graphic format and includes an interactive map. The map shows the most recent listings in red so renters can keep track of what's on the market. It's convenient for tenants as it allows them to check if a property is pet-friendly or if there are amenities they still want.

Rentals.com

Rentals.com helps tenants find the perfect home for them, whether it's a condo, loft, duplex, or duplex.

Rentdigs

This website offers free photo listings. The platform also provides information on how potential tenants can find rent-to, or buy-to-own properties. Rentdigs allows you to upload one photo with a very brief description. So make sure to have a good picture.

Rent.com

This website is meant to promote a substantial number of rental houses. You'll love this site because it has a high traffic. This is a great way to promote your rental property.

Zumper

Zumper, a site with added value, provides neighborhood and city maps for your tenants. Its listings are limited to one photo and only one description, but you can add a detailed description to your property.

Social Media Platforms

Non housing websites can be a powerful tool to promote your rental property listings. Why not share your rental property listing via social media? There will always a place for you to share it. Simply give the most descriptive and optimized description for your property. Facebook, Twitter. Pinterest. Instagram.

Airbnb

Airbnb is an established name in the rental market. It is actually a site for renting homes, which connects homeowners to those looking for short-term rentals. Airbnb is well-known for its ability to share goods or services.

Apartments.com

Apartments.com has a great tool to help you find long-term condo or apartment rentals. The site also offers great deals and offers upfront savings for users who rent through it.

VRBO

VRBO stands For Vacation Rentals from Owners. This platform is well-known as a specialist in apartments and condos.

Nextdoor

This site offers a forum for local areas based on their members' data. This is a useful site for both realtors and property owners who wish to make their services known to the community.

Facebook Groups

Do not take Facebook group membership for granted. Facebook groups offer insights and can help you promote properties. There are more than 500,000,000 Facebook users. Facebook groups also offer highly customizable local search features.

HomeAway

This platform offers rentals of whole properties, as well hostels, rooms, and even bed options. HomeAway, which owns VRBO, uses the site to rent short-term vacation homes of single rooms or partially furnished accommodations.

Walk Score

Walk Score is an additional property management feature. It gives renters the ability to track commute times, transport costs, or Sublet.com information for their property.

Landlords are allowed to post a standard listing without charge. Premium listings may get as many as five hundred times the leads.

Move

This site is a one stop platform that offers many services for buyers and sellers as well as renters. This site allows users to search for exactly the place they are looking for and to rent it. Move has an extensive database of listings available for customers. It boasts a 40 million customer base and provides useful tips about various subjects.

Pet owners

This site provides a nationwide directory of apartments and pet-friendly properties, as well as hotels and apartments. Renters have no obligation to use this website.

Conclusion

Although many people could do with more money, others are not sure what to do. Maybe you need it to pay for travel or buy an item that is beyond your means. Perhaps you also need it to establish an emergency fund. Whatever your reason, it is possible to create passive income streams. It is possible to create passive income streams with enough motivation and perseverance. Do not be afraid to work hard. It is important to remember that when everything is done and the results are visible, you feel proud. This is something to be proud of, isn't he?

In this book we discuss many options for creating steady passive income streams. We talked about passive income streams. These are streams that you can create that will give you money for long periods. Also, we discussed the distinction between passive and active earnings. This is where you earn active income by working actual hours. The IRS plays a different role than active income. They view passive income differently to active income. But, passive income has its benefits. We also examined the benefits that passive income streams can bring to you, including financial stability and time freedom.

In Chapter 2, we looked at how social media can be used to generate passive income streams. It is possible to boost passive income through advertising on YouTube channels and blogging sites. We also spoke about affiliate marketing. In this case, you are able to promote the products and receive compensation. We learned how you can become an affiliate. A company can either contact you to promote your product or you can reach them directly. This can occur especially if their product is relevant to your business.

Chapter 3 focused on dropshipping. Its benefits, including the lack of stock to hand and the possibility to sell products for a good profit. We discovered that the majority of the work associated with dropshipping comes from the company, such stock control, packaging and shipping. We also reviewed how Amazon FBA programs can be used to promote products. A specific niche, which is something you are most interested in, can significantly increase your sales and bring you more profit. We also discussed printing-on-demand. This is an excellent way to promote and market your brand.

In Chapter 4, we covered passive income boosting through the purchase of rental property. We also discussed some of the benefits to owning rental property. These include a steady income and more time for what you should be focusing on. We explored ways that you could increase your property value. This could include adding an additional building that could be rented out for tenants. We also discussed how stock can be invested in. We learned that it takes a lot of research to increase profitability. But, investing in the stock exchange can provide a great opportunity to generate passive income.

In Chapter 5, we conducted an investigation into selling courses online. We discovered that online courses must be engaging, enjoyable, and informative. We also discussed how to keep students satisfied and happy while they are taking these courses. We agreed that you must be present with your students and help them feel important. Peer-tospeer lending was discussed. People often prefer it because it's cheaper to borrow money. We also discussed the various platforms that allow peer-to-peer lending. We discussed the potential risks and suggested ways to minimize them. For example, we could only lend to people who are low-risk.

In Chapter 6, you will learn about other ways to make passive income with the internet. Shutterstock has a way to sell photos. Photos must be of high quality. Cashback apps can be linked to specific stores that offer cashback. We also talked about Instagram sponsored posts in which products are promoted. We also discussed how you can make an app and make money. Also, you can invest in cryptocurrencies, which are the ones that offer the best deals. We were also taught about blockchains and the information that is stored there. We also discussed the possibility of mining for bitcoins. Aside from being able to do complex mathematics and decoding in mining, you also need to have the ability to think for yourself. We also discussed how to sell domain names at a profit and how to get an appraisal for the website. The logo (or brand) that you create for a purchased website is essential in order to increase its value. We researched how to make a podcast, and how it can be made money by advertising. We also found out that Fiverr offers the opportunity to sell your services (which are your areas or expertise).

In Chapter 7, you will learn about the benefits of buying vending devices. We also discussed setting up a laundromat. In order to open a laundromat, you must ensure there is an existing market. You can also make more money by selling products like detergents, sodas, or snacks. We looked at the rewards offered by credit cards. We learned that credit cards come with different rewards. It is important to choose the one that offers the most value for your situation. The topic of renting your vehicle was also brought up. The rental of your car can bring you a steady stream of passive income. However, you should ensure that your car is covered by the appropriate insurance before you let anyone else drive it.

We also looked at the possibility to rent out garage space. It should be legal in your region, and if so it could provide you with a steady passive income stream. We looked at the various things people like to keep, such as classic cars, tools they use for hobbies or equipment for their side business. We discovered that people love convenience and would gladly pay to have their houses cleaned out and store their stuff in your garage.

There are many possibilities for passive income streams. Many of the methods required extensive research. We also realized that no method should be left up to chance. This is why some of these methods require hard labor to get started. But once your passive income source is established and established, it will most likely run by itself with minimal maintenance.

You cannot get anything for nothing. The process of creating a passive stream of income can take some effort. However, when the money begins to flow in, it is possible to sit back and relax while you enjoy the wealth you've worked so hard for.

www.ingramcontent.com/pod-product-compliance
Lightning Source LLC
Chambersburg PA
CBHW050023130526
44590CB00042B/1870